THE MANNERS RELATING TO EATING

Kitāb ādāb al-akl

Book XI of the
Revival of the Religious Sciences

Iḥyā' ʿUlūm al-Dīn

OTHER TITLES IN THE ISLAMIC TEXTS SOCIETY

AL-GHAZĀLĪ SERIES

FROM THE *Iḥyā' ʿulūm al-dīn*

Al-Ghazālī on Invocations & Supplications

Al-Ghazālī on Disciplining the Soul & Breaking the Two Desires

Al-Ghazālī on Patience and Thankfulness

Al-Ghazālī on Love, Longing, Intimacy & Contentment

Al-Ghazālī on the Remembrance of Death & the Afterlife

OTHER WORKS

Al-Ghazālī on the Ninety-Nine Beautiful Names of God

(*al-Maqṣad al-asnā fī sharḥ asmā' Allāh al-ḥusnā*)

Al-Ghazālī Letter to a Disciple

(*Ayyuhā'l-walad*)

AL-GHAZĀLĪ

ON THE MANNERS RELATING TO EATING · *Kitāb ādāb al-akl*

BOOK XI of THE REVIVAL OF THE RELIGIOUS SCIENCES · *Iḥyāʾ ʿulūm al-dīn*

translated with an INTRODUCTION and NOTES by
D. JOHNSON-DAVIES

THE ISLAMIC TEXTS SOCIETY

First published in 2000 by
THE ISLAMIC TEXTS SOCIETY
MILLER'S HOUSE
KINGS MILL LANE
GREAT SHELFORD
CAMBRIDGE CB22 5EN, U.K.

Reprint 2004, 2010, 2012

British Library Cataloguing-in-Publication Data.
A catalogue record for this book is
available from the British Library.

ISBN 978 0946621 72 9 cloth
ISBN 978 0946621 73 6 paper

CONTENTS

Abbreviations VI · Prologue VII
Introduction XI

THE BOOK OF MANNERS RELATING TO EATING

[Prologue 1]

CHAPTER ONE: What is Necessary for the Person Eating Alone 3
Before the Food is Served 3
When One is Eating 7
When the Meal is Over 10

CHAPTER TWO: Additional Manners of Eating When in Company 13

CHAPTER THREE: Manners to be Adopted When Presenting Food to Visiting Brethren 19

CHAPTER FOUR: The Manners of Hospitality 29

A Section Combining Miscellaneous Good Manners and Legal Prohibitions 47

Notes 53

APPENDIX: Persons cited in text 61

Index to Qur'ānic quotations 71

Bibliography 73

General Index 77

ABBREVIATIONS

Al-Aʿlām	:	Ziriklī, *Al-Aʿlām*
Ājurrī	:	al-Ājurrī, *K. al-Sharīʿa*
ʿAṭṭār	:	Arberry (tr.), *Muslim Saints and Mystics*
Azami	:	M.M. Azami, *Studies in Early Hadith Literature*
Dermenghem	:	Dermenghem, *Vies des saints musulmans*
EI	:	*Encyclopaedia of Islam* (First edition)
EI^2	:	*Encyclopaedia of Islam* (Second edition)
Fihrist	:	Ibn al-Nadīm, *K. al-Fihrist*
GALS	:	Brockelmann, *Geschichte … (Supplement)*
GAS	:	Sezgin, *Geschichte …*
Ghāya	:	Ibn al-Jazarī, *Ghāyat al-nihāya …*
Hujwīrī	:	Nicholson (tr.) *Kashf al-maḥjūb*
Iṣāba	:	Ibn Ḥajar, *al-Iṣāba fī tamyīz al-Ṣaḥāba*
Istīʿāb	:	Ibn ʿAbd al-Barr, *al-Istīʿāb fī maʿrifat al-Aṣḥāb*
al-Istīʿāb Mashāhīr	:	Ibn Ḥibbān, *Mashāhīr ʿulamā' al-amṣār*
Q.	:	*al-Qur'ān al-Karīm*
Qushayrī	:	al-Qushayrī, *al-Risāla fī ʿilm al-taṣawwuf*
Ṣafadī	:	al-Ṣafadī, *al-Wāfī bi'l-wafayāt*
SEI	:	*Shorter Encyclopaedia of Islam*
Sulamī	:	al-Sulamī, *Ṭabaqāt al-Ṣūfīya*
Tahdhīb al-Tahdhīb	:	Ibn Ḥajar, *Tahdhīb al-Tahdhīb*
Tārīkh Baghdād	:	al-Khaṭīb al-Baghdādī, *Tārīkh Baghdād*

Prologue

The Book of Manners Relating to Eating (*Kitāb ādāb al-akl*) is the first of the ten books that make up the second Quarter of the *Revival of the Religious Sciences* (*rub*ᶜ *al-*ᶜ*ādāt*). In this Quarter, Ghazālī deals with the norms of conduct in daily life including sexuality and marriage, earning a living, the distinction between what is licit and what is forbidden, friendship and companionship, travelling, music, and *ḥisba*.

Aside from *The Book of Manners Relating to Eating*, the *Revival of the Religious Sciences* contains two other discussions of food. The first of these is in the last book of the same Quarter (*Kitāb ādāb al-ma*ᶜ*īsha wa-akhlāq al-nubuwwa*). This book concludes Ghazālī's treatment of the norms of daily conduct by giving the Prophet Muḥammad's own personal conduct, including his behaviour relating to food, as the surest model for believers to follow. The second discussion is in an altogether different section of the *Revival*, the third Quarter whose subjects are the mortal dangers that face man (*rub*ᶜ *al-muhlikāt*). In the hierarchy of these mortal dangers, the desire for food occupies the first, most serious rank: 'The greatest of the mortal vices which a man may harbour is the desire of the stomach.' Compared with it, even sexual desire comes second. It is in this book, *Kitāb kasr al-shahwatayn*, that the reader will find Ghazālī's deepest ethical and religious analysis, and the justification for his view that the appetite of the stomach is the source of all the other deadly vices. Fortunately, this book of the *Revival* is available in an excellent English edition by Tim Winter (*Al-Ghazali on Disciplining the Soul and on Breaking the Two Desires*, The Islamic Texts Society, Cambridge, 1995).

In reading both *The Book of Manners Relating to Eating* and *Breaking the Two Desires* one is able to see, one the one hand, the motives behind the writing of each of the books, and, on the other hand, the complementary nature of the different books of the *Revival.* The second desire discussed in *Breaking the Two Desires* is sexual desire and what will be necessary once *The Book of Marriage* is translated is a fuller discussion of all these sections together.

By contrast, *The Book of Manners Relating to Eating* has practically none of the complexity and tension that characterize Ghazālī's treatment in *Breaking the Two Desires*, for it has a different purpose. This is simply to provide ordinary believers with a fairly detailed and straightforward model of behaviour. At the core of this model is the living memory of the Prophet's own example, emphasized again in *Kitāb ādāb al-maʿīsha wa-akhlāq al-nubuwwa*, augmented by additional material from the practice of the historical Muslim community. This material can be read elsewhere in Islamic literature; for example, Abū Ṭālib al-Makkī's *Qūt al-qulūb* contains, in chapter 40, an even larger treatment with a greater number of examples. A historian may notice the urban-based nature of this material.

What Ghazālī does in *The Book of Manners Relating to Eating* is to take the available material and turn it into a detailed step by step guidebook for individual believers. For example, what a person ought to do before beginning to eat, in the following exact order: make sure that the food is lawful and lawfully obtained; wash one's hands; place the food on a *sufra* on the floor (like the Prophet used to do, but one may also place it on a table for convenience); sit properly; approach the food with the right intention (namely to maintain one's strength to obey God); be content with what is on offer; and try not to eat alone, instead surrounding oneself with others, a man's own womenfolk and children are specifically mentioned. This is followed by: begin the meal by mentioning the name of God; eat using the right hand; take small mouthfuls, chew well, and swallow completely before taking another mouthful; take from what is closest to one (from the plates on the common table); do not use bread to wipe one's hands; do not blow on hot food, but wait until it cools; do not put one's rejected morsels back on the common plates, etc. The attention to proper manners is designed not to inconvenience or irritate the other persons sharing the food, and the combination of right intention with right practice is the very mark of the Sharīʿa's instructions.

The Book of Manners Relating to Eating is one of the simpler books of the *Revival of the Religious Sciences*. It is for this reason that it helps us see more clearly Ghazālī's plan in the *Revival* as a whole: to survey the development of Islam until his day and to restate the fundamental principles of Islamic belief and practice (often by making explicit what the community had taken for granted) as the essential basis for religious renewal.

Basim Musallam
University of Cambridge
November 1999

INTRODUCTION

IT IS NATURAL that al-Ghazālī's great work, the *Revival of Religious Sciences* (*Iḥyā' ʿUlūm al-Dīn*), covering as it does all aspects of Islamic teaching, should include within its pages a section devoted to manners pertaining to food. As the author points out at the beginning of the '*Book of Manners Relating to Eating*' (*Kitāb ādāb al-akl*), man's service to God and his fidelity to God's purposes are possible only if man has sufficient food to ensure his body and mind can fulfil his duties. Since food is often consumed in company, it is hardly surprising that Islam should have laid down rules and recommendations for eating.

Food being one of the pleasures of life, there are many injunctions against undue indulgence. The general advice is that a person should satisfy his hunger but 'raise his hand' from the food whilst he still has appetite for more. One of the most expressive warnings against gluttony is the *ḥadīth* which says, 'Do not kill your hearts with much eating and drinking, for the heart is like a plant which dies if watered too much.' Islam's recognition that man must experience abstinence in the matter of food, and thus know what it is not to have enough to eat, is expressed by one of its five pillars: the duty of every Muslim to fast during the month of Ramaḍān.

Bread is the staple diet of many peoples, just as it was for the Arabs in the time of the Prophet Muḥammad. For this reason, it has always had special significance, and was honoured by being consumed without *idām*, or condiment. Thus ʿĀ'isha related from the Emissary of God that 'no two sorts of food were joined in a mouthful in the mouth of the Emissary of God (may the blessings and peace of God be upon him): when there was meat there was no bread, when there was bread there was no meat.' Nor should bread be cut with a knife but broken. Furthermore, part of the honour shown to bread is that it should not be thrown away. It is thus common practice in Muslim countries for bread crusts lying in the street to be picked up and placed somewhere out of harm's way. Interestingly, in the colloquial language of Egypt the word *ᶜaysh*—literally, 'life'— is used for 'bread' instead of *khubz*. In Iraq, a country where rice is the staple diet, *ᶜaysh* is used for rice in popular parlance, rather than *ruzz*.

Ghazālī devotes the major part of his *Kitāb ādāb al-akl* to the manners of hospitality. Sharing a meal with others is an opportunity for companionship—it is interesting that in English 'companion' etymologically refers to someone who breaks bread with another. Even before the coming of Islam the obligations owed by a man to his guest were strictly laid down. Similar teachings were enjoined by the Qur'ān and expanded by the *Sunna* of the Prophet. Thus we find numerous examples of *ḥadīth* which deal not only with what would today be termed 'table manners' but also with the host-guest relationship. Many are the stories in ancient Arabic literature that extol the generosity of the host towards his guest. Perhaps the most famous of these are stories about the legendary generosity of Ḥātim al-Ṭā'ī, who went so far as to slaughter his famed horse for lack of anything else with which to feed a guest. Yet Islam, as Ghazālī shows, frowns on unreasonable acts of generosity and ostentation. Thus a host should not put himself out for a guest in such a way as to suffer financial loss. Likewise a guest should not suggest or demand any particular kind of food.

In this connection Ghazālī recounts the amusing story of Salmān al-Fārisī, who presents some guests with whatever he has in the house: no more than some barley bread and coarsely ground salt. One of the visitors suggests that some wild thyme would improve the meal. Therefore, Salmān pawned his ablution bowl to buy some wild thyme. At the end of the meal, the man said, 'Praise be to God who has made us content with what has been provided,' to which Salmān replied, 'Had you been content with what had been provided, my ablution bowl would not be in pawn.'

Generosity should begin with one's own relatives and neighbours. ʿĀ'isha, well aware of the duties she owed her neighbours, was nonetheless anxious to know exactly to which of her neighbours she should give precedence. 'O Emissary of God,' she asked, 'I have two neighbours. With whom shall I begin [by taking food to her]?' He replied, 'Start with the one whose door is nearest to you.'

A well-known *ḥadīth* related by Ibn ʿAbbās expresses what every man should feel towards his fellow man: 'No one is a Muslim who goes to bed sated when his neighbour is hungry and the best way to ensure that he does not go to bed on an empty stomach is to invite him to share your meal with you.'

The famous French gastronome Brillat Savarin expressed well the obligations of a host towards his guest: 'To receive someone as our guest is to be responsible for his happiness the whole time that he is under our roof.' These words sum up what every Muslim instinctively knows to be a sacred duty. 'Happiness' is an all-embracing word and does not merely imply the physical comfort of the guest, and certainly extends far beyond the serving of food to him. It includes making him feel 'at home' and at ease. One of the most famous lines of Arabic poetry says: 'O guest, were you to visit us, you would find that we are the guests and you the householder.' The most delicious of food cannot make up for a guest who does not feel welcome. Thus al-Awzāʿī was asked, 'What is honouring a guest?' His answer: 'A cheerful face.'

The Prophet has shown that everyone, however humble, can be hospitable. A famous *ḥadīth* found in both al-Bukhārī and Muslim, says, 'Food for two is sufficient for three, and the food for three is sufficient for four.' In short, hospitality consists not so much in lavishly entertaining a few people as in having at one's table as many people as possible. Another well-authenticated and oft-quoted *ḥadīth* tells of a man who asked the Prophet, 'Which are the best [practices of Islam]?' The Prophet answered, 'Giving food and greeting people you know and those you do not know.' With these words the Prophet singled out the presentation of food as something in which every Muslim can excel in the practice of his religion.

A host's obligations extend beyond serving food and include not upsetting his guest in any way—for instance, burdening him with sorrows and worries. In his popular compendium *al-Mustaṭraf fī kulli fannin Mustaẓraf*, Abshīhī tells of a man with whom various guests were staying. Unknown to his guests was the accidental death of his young son. The host kept the news to himself in order not to upset his guests, and threatened his wife with divorce if she showed any grief by wailing. When the guests asked where his son was he replied that he was sleeping, and informed them of the news only when they were about to leave. While the story may appear exaggerated to modern ears, it nonetheless illustrates the point that the host and the guest owe each other certain courtesies.

In addition to his normal obligations towards anyone he invites, the host has an almost sacred duty to see that no harm comes to his guest under his roof. Arabic literature abounds with stories of people making all sorts of sacrifices to protect the life of someone who has, in one way or another, become their guest—and a person is a guest once he has eaten your food. A well-known story relates how one of the prisoners awaiting execution protested that they should at least be provided with some food before being put to death. The general then ordered that they be given food. After the men had eaten, one of them reminded the general that, acting as he did, he made them his guests and that he is thus obliged not to harm them.

History tells us, in ʿImād al-Dīn al-Iṣfahānī's words, that at the decisive battle of Hittin several important Christians were taken prisoner, including King Guy, the leader of the Crusader forces, and a certain Reynald of Chatillon. The latter had been guilty of numerous crimes against the Muslims and Saladin had sworn to kill him. The battle was fought on an extremely hot day and the enemy suffered from lack of water. On being brought before Saladin, the King asked for a drink of water. Having drunk, the King passed the cup to Reynald. Immediately, through the interpreter, Saladin made the point that it was the King and not he who had given Reynald the drink of water, thereby confirming that he was under no obligation to his enemy and had not made him a guest by giving him water.

There is *baraka*, or blessing, in eating in company and Ghazālī relates that the Prophet Abraham had the habit of going out in search of persons whom he could invite to his table to share his food. Abraham was once asked how it was that God had taken him as His *khalīl* ('friend'). He answered that it was because of three things, one of which was that he had never had a day or night meal other than with a guest.

'A house in which no guest enters is not entered by the angels.' In this *ḥadīth* the Prophet Muḥammad summed up Islam's attitude towards man's obligation to be hospitable towards his fellows. It is said that ʿAbd Allāh ibn ʿAbbās was the first person to place tables on the roadside for people to eat—a charitable practice honoured today by eminent individuals who set up tables, known as *mawā'id al-Raḥmān* ('the tables of the Merciful'), at appropriate sites in their city where less fortunate folk can break their fast during the month of Ramaḍān.

Ghazālī is concerned with the duties not only of the host but of the guest. These include the general behaviour which begins with accepting the invitation of the host. A person should, where possible, accept every invitation. On this subject a prophetic *ḥadīth* states that 'he who refuses an invitation has shown disobedience to God Almighty and His Prophet.' In particular one should not refuse the invitation of someone because of his poverty or lack of social standing, or because he lives too far away. Ghazālī contends that even while fasting—

except during Ramaḍān—one should accept an invitation to a meal and break the fast, for by bringing joy to a fellow Muslim's heart one receives the same reward.

A man famed for his impeccable manners was asked how he had gained them. He answered: 'Journeying obliged me to visit people; those of their qualities I admired I followed; those I found unpleasant I avoided.' These words encapsulate how a pattern of good manners is established in society. The details may differ—some eat with their hands, others with knives and forks, and yet others with chopsticks. But the aim is one: to observe the general principles of cleanliness and not to upset the person with whom one happens to share the meal. It is just these principles, simple yet abiding, that Islam has followed when establishing proper behaviour for the guest and the host, as they perform the 'rite' of meal-sharing.

Finally, I would like to record very special thanks to my friend Abdurrahman Fitzgerald for his general encouragement and invaluable help in tracing the sources of the Prophetic Traditions, preparing the index and making additions to the appendix. I would also like to express my thanks to T. J. Winter; the present appendix being mostly based on his appendix to *Al-Ghazālī The Remembrance of Death and the Afterlife*.

THE BOOK OF MANNERS RELATING TO EATING

Being the First Book of the Quarter of the Norms of Daily Life (ʿ*Ādāt*)

[PROLOGUE]

In the Name of God, Most Compassionate and Merciful

THANKS BE TO God who has well devised the universe, created the earth and the heavens and sent down sweet water from the clouds. And by the clouds He brought forth grain and herbage. He measured the sustenance [required] and the foods [available], bracing the strength of animals with edible things; and through the eating of food has aided obedience and [the performance of] good works. May the blessings of God be upon Muḥammad, worker of splendid miracles, and upon his Family and Companions—blessings continuous growing ever more with the passage of time, and may He grant him peace.

Now, the goal of those with understanding is to meet God Exalted in the abode of reward. But there is no way to meet God without knowledge and deed, and it is impossible to devote oneself to these without a healthy body. The health of the body is attained only through food and the partaking of food in necessary quantities over periods of time. On this matter, one of the pious *salaf* (predecessors)[A] has said: 'Eating is part of religion.' The Lord

[A] *Salaf*, or 'predecessors', is generally taken to mean the first two generations of Muslims.

of the Worlds, who is the most truthful of speakers, has alluded to this in His words, '*Eat of the good things and do right.*'[1]

Thus he who partakes of food, that he may be aided thereby in knowledge and deeds, and strengthened in piety, should not allow himself to lose control—giving himself the liberties of beasts at pasture. For that which is a means of access to religion must make manifest to him the lights of religion. And the lights of religion are its manners and uses. The servant of God clings to their bridle, the god-fearing man employs them as a bit. Thus may he weigh the appetite for food on the scales of religious law, both when pursuing his appetite and when abstaining from it. Food then becomes something by which to repel sin and acquire recompense, though in the appetite for food the fullest portion is for the self.

The Prophet (may God bless him and grant him peace) has said: 'A man is rewarded even for the morsel he raises to his mouth and to the mouth of his wife,'[2] it being so only if he raises it in accordance with religion and for its sake, observing therein its manners and functions.

We shall now indicate the functions of religion in eating, the religious duties, uses and manners of eating, its good morality and modes—in four chapters, with a section at the end.

CHAPTER ONE: The manners which the eater must observe when eating alone.

CHAPTER TWO: The additional manners of eating in company.

CHAPTER THREE: Relating to the preparation of food for visiting brethren.

CHAPTER FOUR: Relating to giving an invitation, hospitality and the like.

CHAPTER ONE

What is Necessary for the Person Eating Alone

Being three sections:
before the food is served; when one is eating;
when the meal is over.

On the manners to be observed before the meal and they are:
The first [rule of conduct]: that the food be lawful both in itself and in the means by which it was acquired; that it shall be in accordance with the *Sunna*[A] and with piety. It should not have been gained through anything contrary to canonical law, nor through some evil inclination, nor deceit relating to debt—and agreeing with what will be presented in the *Book of the Lawful and the Unlawful*[B] regarding the meaning of what is unconditionally good.

God has ordered the eating of that which is good (*al-ṭayyib*), this being the lawful. He has put the prohibition of 'wrongful eating' (*al-akl bi'l-bāṭil*)[C] before that of killing, in order to illustrate the gravity of that which is unlawful and the greatness of the blessing of that which is lawful. He said, '*O you who believe, squander not your wealth (lā ta'kulū amwālakum)*[D] *among yourselves in vanity...And kill not one another,*'[3] to the end of the verse. The basic principle with respect to food is that food must be good, this

[A] The sayings and actions of the Prophet.

[B] The fourteenth book of the *Iḥyā'* and the fourth of the quarter of the Norms of Daily Life (*ʿĀdāt*).

[C] In Arabic, *al-akl bi'l bāṭil* means acquiring anything unlawfully.

[D] *Ta'kulū* is from the same root as *akl*.

being one of the duties and fundamentals of religion.

The second [rule of conduct] is to wash one's hands. The Emissary of God (may God bless him and grant him peace) has said, 'Ablution performed before a meal banishes poverty, ablution after a meal banishes minor sins.'[4] And in another version, '[Ablution performed] both before and after the meal banishes poverty.' Since the hand cannot escape dirt in the performance of tasks, washing it is the best way to keep it clean and unsullied. And because eating as a support for religion is a form of worship, it is proper that one approach it in the same state as for prayers.

The third [rule of conduct] is to place the food on a *sufra*[A] on the ground—for this is closest to what the Emissary of God (may God bless him and grant him peace) did—rather than to place it on a raised table. 'When food was brought to the Emissary of God (may God bless him and grant him peace), he would place it on the ground,'[5] for this is closer to humility. If not, then it should be on a *sufra*, as a reminder of travelling;[B] and travelling puts in mind travelling to the Afterlife and the need for provision in the form of pious deeds. Anas ibn Mālik said, 'The Emissary of God (may God bless him and grant him peace) ate neither on a table (*khiwān*) nor in a *sukurruja*.'[C] Someone asked: 'On what have you been eating, then?' 'On a *sufra*,' he said.[6]

It was said that after [the death of] the Emissary of God four things were introduced: tables, sieves, potash,[D] and repletion. Know that although we have said that eating on a *sufra* is more appropriate, we do not say that eating on a table is proscribed as either distasteful or forbidden, for no proscription of it has been established. As for the claim that it was an innovation[7] that occurred after the Emissary of God, not everything innovated is

[A] A ground cover, generally made of leather, which was carried on journeys and spread out for meals.

[B] *Sufra* has the same root (*sfr*) as words denoting travel.

[C] *Sukurruja* is an arabicised Persian word for a bowl-shaped vessel.

[D] *Ushnān*: a substance with which clothes and hands were cleaned.

proscribed, but only that innovation which is contrary to an established *Sunna*, as it does away with the canonical law while not solving the problem. However, innovation may be required in cases where the circumstances have changed. For there is nothing about a table other than that food has been raised from the floor and laid out on it for facility of eating and the like. And there is nothing abhorrent about this.

The four things together regarded as innovation are not of equal importance. Potash is good because of its cleansing properties. Washing is desirable for cleanliness and potash perfects cleaning. People had not been using potash perhaps because they were not accustomed to doing so, or it was not easily available, or they were preoccupied with matters more important than indulging in excessive cleanliness. Thus they also used not to wash their hands [before and after meals], their [only drying] cloth being the hollow in the soles of their feet. This, however, does not preclude the desirability of washing.

As for the sieve, its purpose is to render food more pleasant. This is permissible so long as it does not lead to a life of excessive luxury. Just as the table is helpful in eating, it, too, is permissible so long as it does not lead to pride and haughtiness. Repletion is the worst of the four in that it arouses the passions and activates maladies in the body. Therefore, understand the difference between these innovations.

The fourth [rule of conduct] is that upon sitting at the *sufra* one ought to sit properly and remain in that position. Thus, 'The Emissary of God (may God bless him and grant him peace) used often to squat down on his knees and sit on his heels for the meal. At other times he would raise his right leg and sit on his left.' He used to say: 'I do not eat when reclining[8]...for I am but a slave; I eat as a slave eats and sit as a slave sits.'[9]

To drink when reclining is also disagreeable for the stomach, and to eat lying down or reclining is abhorrent except when munching seeds and berries. It was related concerning ʿAlī (may God ennoble his countenance) that he ate dry bread from a shield while lying down—[in another version], while lying prostrate on his stomach, which the Bedouin Arabs sometimes did.

The fifth [rule of conduct] is to have the intention, when eating, of strengthening oneself in obedience to God, so as to be obedient through food and not to seek gratification and luxurious living through food. Ibrāhīm ibn Shaybān said, 'For eighty years I have not eaten anything for my own appetite.' And yet he resolved to lessen his intake of food. Since he ate for the purpose of increasing his capacity for worship, his intention was sincere only when he ate less than what satisfied him, for repletion obstructs worship and does not increase the capacity for it. Thus for this intention it is necessary that one's appetite be broken, and that one prefer frugality to being distended.

The Emissary of God (may God bless him and grant him peace) said, 'No human being has ever filled a container worse than his own stomach. The son of Adam needs no more than some morsels of food to keep up his strength; doing so, he should consider that a third of [his stomach] is for food, a third for drink and a third for breathing.'[10]

With regard to this intention, the person must refrain from stretching his hand towards the food unless he is hungry, for hunger is something which must always precede eating. Then he must raise up his hand before repletion. Doing so, he dispenses with doctors. The benefit of eating little and of gradually reducing one's food intake will be dealt with in the 'Chapter of Destroying the Appetite for Food',[11] from the fourth section of those things that bring about a man's end.

The sixth [rule of conduct] is to be content with any sustenance and any food available. One should not strive for luxury, ask for more or expect a condiment[A] in which to dip one's bread. In fact, it is a mark of the esteem accorded to bread that no condiment be served with it.

One Tradition[12] enjoins holding bread in esteem, for every-

[A] *Udm* or *idām* refers to something eaten with bread.

thing that keeps the spark of life alive and strengthens one's capacity for worship is of great benefit and should not be despised. In fact, when the time for prayer arrives, one should not put off eating bread [i.e., the meal] if there is sufficient time. The Emissary of God (may God bless him and grant him peace) said, 'If the time for evening prayers and that of supper coincide, begin with the supper.'[13] ᶜAbd Allāh Ibn ᶜUmar would often hear the Imām reciting [the Qur'ān at prayers] and would not rise from his supper. So long as one does not yearn for food and there is no harm in putting off the time for food, it is more seemly to give preference to prayer. But if the food is ready and the time for prayer has come, and by putting off the meal the food will become cold or spoiled, giving it preference is more desirable when there is time, whether one craves it or not—according to most Traditions. This is because one cannot abstain from thinking about food that has been laid out, even when it is not very hungry.

The seventh [rule of conduct] is that one should try to have many hands partake of the meal, even if they be only your women and children. The Emissary of God (may God bless him and grant him peace) said, 'Gather together over your food and you will be blessed in it.'[14] Anas [ibn Mālik] said, 'The Emissary of God (may God bless him and grant him peace) used not to eat alone.'[15] And the Emissary of God said, 'The best food is that over which there are many hands.'[16]

On the manners to be observed when eating

One should begin the meal with the words 'In the name of God'[17] and end it with 'Praise be to God'.[18] It would be well if one were to say with every mouthful 'In the name of God', that greed may not distract one from mentioning the name of God (Exalted be He!). One should say with the first mouthful 'In the name of God', with the second 'In the name of God the Merciful', with the third 'In the name of God the Merciful, the Compassionate'—and loudly to remind others.

A person should eat with the right hand,[19] commencing and ending with salt.[20] He should keep each mouthful small and chew it well. He should not stretch out his hand for another mouthful before swallowing the first, for eating this way would be too hasty. Moreover, he should not decry any [food] being eaten. The Prophet found no fault in anything he ate; if he liked something he ate it, otherwise he left it alone.[21]

A man should eat of that which is closest to him, save in the case of fruit, where he may let his hand rove around and choose. The Emissary of God (may God bless him and grant him peace) said, 'Eat of that which is close to you.'[22] Then he circled round the fruit with his hand. He was asked about this and he said, 'It is not all of one sort.'[23]

A person should not eat from the rim of the bowl nor yet from the centre.[24] He should eat from the circumference of the loaf—unless it is only a small loaf which should be broken instead of cut with a knife.[25] Meat, too, is not to be cut. [The Emissary of God] forbade it, saying: 'Tear it into pieces.'[26] Neither a dish nor anything else ought to be placed on bread; only that which is eaten with it [may be placed on it]. The Prophet said, 'Hold bread in esteem for God (Exalted be He!) has sent it down as one of Heaven's blessings.'[27] Thus one should not wipe one's hand with bread. He (may God bless him and grant him peace) said, 'If a morsel falls from one of you, let him pick it up and remove what is harmful from it—let him not leave it for Satan. He should not wipe his hand with a cloth until he has licked his fingers, for he knows not which part of his food contains the blessing.'[28]

And one must not blow on hot food. This is prohibited. One should wait patiently until it is easy to eat.[29]

Of dates a person should eat an odd number: seven, eleven, or twenty-one, or however many they may come to. He must not place the dates and their stones together in one dish, or bring them together in the palm of the hand, but should place the stones from his mouth to the back of his hand and then discard them. Anything that has a kernel or dregs should be dealt with similarly. Any food found distasteful must be left with the dregs rather than put aside in the dish, lest it mislead anyone into eating it.

A person should not drink much while eating unless he has choked on a mouthful or is truly thirsty, for it has been said that this is medically desirable, it being stomachic.[A]

As for the manners of drinking, one should take the jug in the right hand,[30] say 'In the name of God' and drink it in sips rather than in gulps. The Emissary of God (may God bless him and grant him peace) said, 'Drink water in sips, do not gulp it down—for liver ailments are brought about by gulping.'[31] Do not drink either standing up or lying down, for the Emissary of God (may God bless him and grant him peace) forbade drinking while standing. It was related that sometimes he drank standing up; but he no doubt had a good excuse for doing so.[32]

A person should be careful about the bottom of the jug lest it drip on him; and he should look into the jug before drinking. He should neither belch nor breathe into the jug,[33] but move it away from his mouth, saying 'Praise be to God', and handing it back with the words 'In the name of God'.[34]

After drinking, the Emissary of God (may God bless him and grant him peace) said, 'Praise be to God who has made it sweet and wholesome through His mercy, and has not made it salty and bitter with our sins.'[35]

The jug and everything that is passed around to people should be passed to the right. The Emissary of God (may God bless him and grant him peace) was drinking some milk with Abū Bakr on his left, a bedouin on his right and ʿUmar alongside him. ʿUmar said, 'Give it to Abū Bakr'—and the bedouin passed it over. The Emissary of God said, 'To the right, then to the right.'[36] And he would drink in three swallows,[37] saying 'Praise be to God' after each one and 'In the name of God' before. After the first swallow he would say 'Praise be to God', after the second he would add

[A] That is, not drinking a lot of water helps digestion.

'Lord of the Worlds', after the third 'the Merciful, the Compassionate.'[38]

The above amounts to nearly twenty ways of behaving when eating and drinking for which the Narrations and Traditions of God's Emissary furnish evidence.[A]

What is recommended after eating

One should hold back before becoming replete, and lick one's fingers, wipe them with a cloth, wash them and pick up the [fallen] crumbs of food. The Emissary of God (may God bless him and grant him peace) said, 'He who eats what has fallen from the table shall live in comfort and his children shall be kept healthy.'[39]

A person should use a tooth-stick but should not swallow what he extracts from his teeth with tooth-sticks except what he can collect from the base of his teeth with his tongue. Whatever he extracts with tooth-sticks must be discarded, and he should rinse [his mouth] after using tooth-sticks—for about this there is a Tradition on the authority of the family of the Prophet.[40]

One should also lick the dish and drink any liquid in it. It is said that he who licks the dish, washes it clean and drinks the liquid shall have the reward of someone who has manumitted a slave;[41] and that the picking up of crumbs is the dowries of houris. And that a person should thank God wholeheartedly for what He has given him to eat, and regard this food as a favour from Him.

God has said: '*Eat of the good things with which We have provided you and give thanks to God.*'[42] Whenever one has eaten lawful food one should say, 'Praise be to God through whose bounty good deeds are accomplished and blessings brought down. O God, nourish us with what is good and make us act virtuously.' If a person eats something dubious, then he should say, 'Praise be to God in any event. O God, do not make this something that

[A] *Al-Akhbār wa'l-āthār* ('Narrations and Traditions'). According to Lane, these two terms are generally held to be synonymous, though *āthār* often stands for something related by a Companion of the Prophet rather than the Prophet himself.

strengthens our disobedience to You.'

After eating, a person should recite '*Say, God is One*' and '*For the taming of the Quraysh*'.[43] And he must not rise from the table until it has first been cleared. If he eats food [prepared] by someone, he should offer these words of supplication: 'O God, increase his benefit; bless for him that with which You have provided him; make it easy for him to do good through it; make him satisfied with what You have given him; and make him and us grateful.' If he has broken the fast at someone's house, then let him say: 'May those fasting break their fast with you, and may the pious eat your food, and may the angels pray for you.'[44]

He should constantly ask God for forgiveness and grieve over anything dubious he may have eaten, so as to extinguish, through tears and grief, the heat of the Fire to which he is exposed—this by grace of the Prophet's words, 'The Fire is most fitting for every piece of flesh that has originated from what is unlawful.'[45] One who eats [something unlawful] and weeps [in regret] is not like one who eats and is oblivious.

Let him who has drunk milk say: 'O God, bless us in what You have provided for us and grant us its increase.' When a person eats something else, he should say: 'O God, bless us in what You have provided for us and grant us something better.' In the [former] supplication the Emissary of God (may God bless him and grant him peace) singled out milk for its overall benefit.[46]

It is recommended that after eating one should say: 'Praise be to God who has given us food, drink and sufficiency, and who has sheltered us. O our Master and Lord, You who defend us from all, whose divine decree nothing can countermand; You have appeased hunger and protected [us] from fear. And so to You be praise. You have given refuge to the orphaned and shown the right path from the wrong; You have relieved people from impoverishment—to You then be praise, praise that is plentiful, everlasting, good, profitable and blessed. For You are worthy and deserving of it. O God, You have fed us with the good things, so make us act virtuously, and let this help us be obedient to You. We take refuge in You should we make use [of food] in our disobedience to You.'

As for the washing of the hands with potash, the way to do it is to place the potash in the left palm, to wash the three fingers of the right hand first, to strike the fingers against the dry potash and to wipe one's lips with it. After this, one should wash one's mouth with one's finger, rubbing the front and back parts of the teeth, the palate and the tongue. Then, one should wash the potash from one's fingers with water. With the remainder of the dry potash one should rub one's fingers, back and front. By doing this one is able to dispense with putting more potash on the mouth and having to re-wash it.

CHAPTER TWO

Additional Manners of Eating When in Company

They are seven [in number]:

The first [rule of conduct] is that we must not begin eating when someone else present deserves precedence, by reason of age or superiority for they must be followed and emulated. Once this is observed, [people] should not be made to wait long if they are eager to eat and have gathered together for [that purpose].

The second [rule of conduct] is that they should not be silent over the food, for that is the custom of the Persians. They ought to converse amicably and relate the stories of the pious on food and other subjects.

The third [rule of conduct] is that a person should be courteous to his companion with whom he shares the dish. When the meal is a shared one, he should not aim to eat more than another does; this is forbidden except with the consent of his companion. Rather, the aim ought to be to show him preference. One must not eat two dates at one time unless [the other guests] have done so or unless one has asked their permission.[47]

If a companion has reduced his consumption of food, one should encourage him and awaken his appetite for the food by urging him to eat. But one must not say 'eat' more than three times, for that would be importunate and excessive.

When the Emissary of God (may God bless him and grant him peace) was spoken to about something three times, he was not addressed again after that. He himself would repeat himself three times, and it is not good manners to do more than this.[48]

It is forbidden to swear an oath that someone shall eat. Al-Ḥasan the son of ʿAlī said, 'Food is too trivial a thing to be the subject of an oath.'

The fourth [rule of conduct] is that a person should not oblige his companion to ask him to eat. A certain man of letters said, 'The best of those who eat is he who does not force his friend to keep watch over him as he eats and who relieves his brother of the trouble of speaking.'

A person need not leave something he desires because someone else has looked at it, for that would be affectation. He should proceed normally, without diminishing in the least the conduct he is used to when alone. He must accustom himself to being good-mannered when alone in order to avoid showing affectation in company. It would be good were he to reduce his food as a sign of affection for his brethren, to look at them and see when they are in need—for this is sound. There is no harm in eating more with the intention of helping and stimulating people's ardour for food; in fact it is good.

[ʿAbd Allāh] ibn al-Mubārak used to serve superb fresh dates to his brethren and say, 'To him who eats the most I shall give a dirham for each stone.' He used to count the stones and to give anyone who had the most date-stones an equal number of dirhams. He did this to dispel shyness and increase the capacity for enjoyment.

Jaʿfar ibn Muḥammad (may God be pleased with both of them) said, 'My most beloved brethren are those who eat the most and take the biggest mouthfuls. The most disagreeable one is he who forces me to pay attention to him when he eats.' All this is an indication that one should proceed normally and eschew affectation. Jaʿfar also said: 'The quality of a man's love for his brother is shown by the quality of the food in his house.'

The fifth [rule of conduct] is that there is nothing wrong in washing one's hands in a basin. And if he has eaten alone, he may clear his throat in it. However, this should not be done if he has eaten with others. When someone offers a person the basin out of respect, then let him accept it. Anas ibn Mālik and Thābit al-Bunānī sat together at a meal when Anas offered the latter a basin. Thābit declined it, to which Anas said, 'If your brother shows you respect, then accept his respect and do not refuse it, for God Himself [Great and Glorious is He] shows respect.'

It is related that Hārūn al-Rashīd had invited Muᶜāwiya's blind father. Al-Rashīd poured water over his hands into the basin, and when he had finished he asked, 'O father of Muᶜāwiya, do you know who poured the water over your hands?' He said, 'No.' Al-Rashīd said, 'It was the Commander of the Faithful.' He said, 'O Commander of the Faithful, you have shown respect for learning and have revered it. May God [grant you] reverence and show you respect in the same way that you have revered learning and those who pursue it.'

There is nothing wrong in [people] washing [their] hands together in a basin at one and the same time, for this is more allied to humility and reduces the necessity for waiting. If everyone has not done so, then it is not necessary to pour the water for each person separately. The water may be collected in the basin. The Emissary of God (may God bless him and grant him peace) said, 'Unite in your ablution and God will unite your state of disunion.'[49] It is said that this was what was intended.

ᶜUmar ibn ᶜAbd al-ᶜAzīz wrote [instructions] for the big cities saying, 'Basins are not to be lifted up in front of people unless they are full, and do not copy the Persians.' Ibn Masᶜūd said, 'Unite when washing the hands in a single basin, and do not follow the practice of the Persians.'

Some have preferred the servant pouring water over a person's hands to sit rather that stand as this is closer to humility; while others may dislike his sitting. It was related that a servant who was seated poured water over the hands of a person. The one on whom water was poured stood up. He was asked, 'Why have you stood up?' He replied, 'One of us should be standing.'

This is more appropriate, for it is easier for pouring and for washing, and more allied to the humility of the person who pours [the water]. If he intends to do so, then letting him perform this service implies no arrogance, since the practice is common.

Regarding the basin, there are seven rules of good manners. One should not spit into it; those behind should give precedence [to those in front]; a person should accept the respect which another shows him by giving him precedence; the basin should be moved to the right; a group of people should share it; the water in it should be collected; the servant must stand; in rinsing the mouth let the water fall from the hand gently to avoid splashing the attendant or the companions; and the master of the house must himself pour the water over the hands of his guest. This is what Mālik [ibn Anas] did for al-Shāfiʿī when he first stayed with him. He said to him, 'Do not let what you have seen me do alarm you, for to serve a guest is a religious duty.'

The sixth [rule of conduct] is that a person should not look at his companions or watch them eating lest they be embarrassed; he should avert his gaze from them and be preoccupied with himself. He must not refrain from eating before his brethren have finished, for they will feel diffident about eating after he is done. He should instead stretch out his hand and take hold of a little food and eat of it until they have had their fill. If he is a light eater, he ought to stop at the beginning and to lessen the food he takes, until they have made themselves at home with the food; and then he can at last eat with them. Many of the Companions used to do this. If for some reason he stops eating, however, he must apologise to them so as to put them at ease.

The seventh [rule of conduct] is to do nothing which others hold to be unclean. Thus a person should not shake his hand in the dish [to remove any food clinging to it] nor move his head towards the dish when placing the morsel in his mouth. If he removes something from his mouth he should avert his face from the food and take it out with his left hand. He must not immerse a greasy morsel in the vinegar, nor the vinegar in the greasy portion, for others may not like this. He should not immerse in the broth or the vinegar what is left of any morsel he has cut with his teeth; nor should he talk about things that bring to mind things held to be unclean.

CHAPTER THREE

Manners to be Adopted When Presenting Food to Visiting Brethren

PRESENTING FOOD TO brethren has much merit. Jaʿfar ibn Muḥammad said, 'If you are seated with brethren at a table, make it a long session, for it is a span of time which is not counted from your lives.'

Al-Ḥasan [al-Baṣrī] said, 'A man shall be definitely accountable for every expenditure he makes on himself, his parents and others less closely related—that is, except what he spends on his brethren for food; for God would be embarrassed to ask him about that.' There are [also other] Traditions about providing food for people.

The Emissary of God (may God bless him and grant him peace) said, 'The angels continue to pray for every one of you as long as his table is set before him, until it is taken away.'[50] It has been related that a certain scholar of Khurāsān used to present his brethren with so much food that they were unable to eat it all. He would say, 'We have been informed that the Emissary of God (may God bless him and grant him peace) said, "When brethren have raised their hands from the food, he who eats from what is left over is not accountable."[51] And so, I present much food to you that we may eat what is left over.'

In a Tradition it is said, 'The servant of God is not accountable for what he eats with his brethren.'[52] For this reason, some used to over-eat when in company and eat little on their own. In a Tradition it is said, 'There are three things for which a servant of God is not accountable: the meal of *suḥūr*,[A] what he breaks his fast

[A] The light meal eaten before the fasting day of Ramaḍān begins.

with and what he eats with brethren.'[53]

ʿAlī (may God be pleased with him) said, 'For me to bring my brethren together to a *ṣāʿ*[A] of food is dearer to me than manumitting a slave.' Ibn ʿUmar (may God be pleased with both of them) used to say, 'An indication of someone's generosity is the quality of the provisions he takes on his journey and what he has expended for his companions.'

The Companions used to say, 'Gathering together over food is one of the traits of noble character.'[B] They used to gather together to recite the Qur'ān and would disperse only when they had received knowledge for their minds, as they do food and drink for their bodies. It was said, 'The gathering together of brethren with sufficient food, sociability and congeniality is not of this world.'[C]

In a Tradition it is said, 'God (Exalted is He!) says to the servant on the Day of Resurrection: "O son of Adam, I was hungry and you fed Me not." And he will say, "How shall I feed You when You are the Lord of the Worlds?" And He will say, "Your Muslim brother was hungry and you fed him not, and had you fed him you would have fed Me."'[54]

The Emissary of God (may God bless him and grant him peace) said, 'If a visitor comes to you, be generous in your hospitality to him.'[55] He said, 'In Paradise there are rooms from inside which the exterior can be viewed, and from outside which the interior can be viewed; they are for the soft-spoken who have provided food for people and prayed at night when people were asleep.'[56]

[A] A unit of measurement which can vary. A *ṣāʿ* of grain, for example, is the amount that can be taken four times with both hands held in the shape of a bowl.

[B] *Makārim al-akhlāq* ('noble character') is an expression which appears in Bukhārī, Manāqib, 3572 and in Muslim, Faḍā'il al-Ṣaḥāba, 4521. Before embracing Islam, Abū Dharr asked his brother to go and see about 'this man who says he is a prophet.' His brother returned and said, 'I saw him enjoining noble character upon people.' The word *ḥusn* ('excellence' or 'beauty') is sometimes substituted for *makārim* ('noble traits'), as in the *Muwaṭṭa'* of Mālik: 'I have been brought forth to perfect beauty of character.'

[C] That is, it is not like any worldly happiness.

He said, 'The best of you are those who have provided food.'[57] And he said, 'He who has given food to his brother to satisfy him and given him drink to quench his thirst, God has distanced him from Hell by seven ditches—the distance between each two ditches is what can be walked in five hundred years.'[58]

The rules of conduct are divided between those relating to entering [people's] houses and those relating to the presentation of food.

As for entering [people's house], it is not part of the *Sunna* to visit people during their meal expecting to be fed. This is to take them by surprise and has been forbidden. God (Exalted be He!), has said: '*Enter not the houses of the Emissary of God unless permission is granted to you to attend a meal, without waiting about for it to be ready*'[59]—that is to say, waiting for the time of the meal and for it to be properly cooked.

One Tradition says, 'He who walks towards food to which he has not been invited has walked as a transgressor and eaten unlawfully.'[60] The right thing for a person to do upon entering—if he does not come expecting food but chances upon [the people of the house] at their meal—is not to eat unless given permission to do so. If the person is told to eat, he should consider the matter, and if he realises that [his hosts] are saying it affectionately to assist him, then he should allow himself to be helped. But if they were saying it because of bashfulness, he should not eat but excuse himself. If, however, he is hungry, betakes himself to one of his brethren so that he may feed him and does not just descend upon him at his meal time—there is no harm in that.

The Emissary of God (may God bless him and grant him peace), Abū Bakr and ʿUmar went to the house of Abu'l-Haytham ibn al-Tayyihān and [the house of] Abū Ayyūb al-Anṣārī in order to eat some food, because they were hungry.[61] Entering in this fashion assists a Muslim to be rewarded for feeding people, and this was the custom of the *salaf*. ʿAwn ibn ʿAbd Allāh al-Masʿūdī had three hundred and sixty friends whom he would visit in the course of a year. Another man had thirty friends whom he would visit in the course of a month; and another had seven friends whom he would visit in the course of a week. Their brethren represent their 'fixed income' in place of 'earnings'. Their hosts provided for them with the purpose of asking their blessings and [this] was an act of worship for [the hosts].

Thus if someone enters [a house], fails to find the master of the house but is confident of his friendship, knowing his joy were he to eat of his food, he may eat without seeking permission—for seeking permission is to gain approval, especially where meals are concerned, where they are free. Many a man has expressly granted his permission and given his oath, [while in reality] unwilling; he thereby renders the eating of his food reprehensible. On the other hand, many an absent man has not given permission and yet the eating of his food is desirable.

God (Exalted be He!) has said '*or your friend*'.[62] The Emissary of God (may God bless him and grant him peace) entered the house of Burayra and ate of her food while she was absent, but the food was from what she had set aside for charity, and he said, 'The charity has arrived at its destination'[63]—since he knew the joy she would feel about it. Therefore, it is possible to enter a house without asking permission, it being sufficient to know that permission would be granted. If one did not know this, one would have to ask permission first, then enter.

Muḥammad ibn Wāsiᶜ and his friends used to enter the house of al-Ḥasan [al-Baṣrī] to eat what they found without permission. When al-Ḥasan came in and saw this, he was happy about it and used to say, 'We were once like that.'

It is related that al-Ḥasan once stood as he ate from the wares of a grocer in the market, taking from this jar a fig and from that a dried date. Hishām[64] said to him, 'O Abū Saᶜīd,[A] how do you reconcile piety with eating the wares of this man without permission?' He said, 'O foolish one, recite to me the verse of food,' and he recited it to him up to the Almighty's words '*or of your friend*'.[65] Hishām asked, 'And who is the friend, O Abū

[A] The patronymic of Ḥasan al-Baṣrī.

Saᶜīd?' He said, 'He with whom the soul is at ease and the heart at rest.'

Some people walked to the house of Sufyān al-Thawrī. They did not find him, so they opened the door, took down the *sufra* and began to eat. Al-Thawrī entered, saying, 'You remind me of the characteristics of the *salaf*—they were like this.'

Some people visited one of the *tābiᶜūn*,[A] who had nothing to put before them. Therefore, he went to the house of one of his brethren but could not find him. He entered, looked at a pot of food the latter had cooked, some bread he had baked and other things, took them all with him, presented them to his friends and told them to eat. When the owner of the house came and saw nothing there, someone told him, 'So-and-so has taken it.' He said, 'He has done well,' and when he met him he said, 'Brother, if they return, then return [here], for these are the manners for entering someone's house.'

Regarding the manners for presenting food, the first [rule of good conduct] is that one refrains from any affectation and presents what is available. If he has nothing available, and he possesses nothing, he should not seek a loan for that purpose, for this would cause him difficulties. If he has available what is necessary for his own consumption and his nature does not allow him to present it, then he need not do so. A man once entered upon an ascetic[66] as he ate. The ascetic said, 'Had I not become indebted to acquire this, I would have fed you from it.'

One of the *salaf* said in explaining affectation, 'It is to feed your brother something that you yourself do not eat, aspiring [to appear] greater in quality and worth.' Al-Fuḍayl [ibn ᶜIyāḍ] used to say, 'People come to be on bad terms with each other only through affectation. One of them invites his brother and puts himself out for him, preventing him from coming back to him.' A man said, 'I do not care which of my brethren comes

[A] *Tābiᶜūn*, or 'those who followed'—in Mecca and Medina, the first generation of Muslims after the Prophet.

to me, for I do not put myself out for him. I merely present what I have, and had I put myself out for him, I would dislike his coming and would tire of him.'

Another man said, 'I used to go to the house of one of my brethren and he would put himself out for me. I said to him, "You do not eat this when you are alone, nor do I. Why, then, do you think that, meeting up with each other, we should eat it? Either you stop this affectation or I shall stop visiting you." He stopped his affectation and for this reason we continued to meet.'

An aspect of affectation is to present all that one has [to one's guest], thereby harming one's children and upsetting them. It was related that a man invited ʿAlī, who said, 'I shall accept your invitation on three conditions: that you bring nothing from the market, that you are not niggardly in what you keep in the house and that you do not harm your children.' One person used to present everything that was in the house, and would not leave any type of food without presenting some of it. Someone else stated, 'We went into the house of Jābir ibn ʿAbd Allāh and he presented us with bread and vinegar, saying, "If we had not proscribed for ourselves affectation, I would have put myself out for you."'

Another said, 'If someone comes for a visit, present what there is; if you are asked to pay someone a visit, do not leave the food and do not let anything remain.' Salmān [al-Fārisī] said, 'The Emissary of God (may God bless him and grant him peace) ordered us not to put ourselves out for a guest with something we did not have, but to present him with what we had.'[67]

In a Tradition about the Prophet Jonah (may God bless him and grant him peace), it is said that when Jonah's brethren visited him, he presented them with small pieces of bread and cut up some greens he had cultivated. Then he told them, 'Eat. Had God not cursed those who incommoded themselves, I would have incommoded myself for you.' On the authority of Anas ibn Mālik and other Companions, it is said that [people] used to present such pieces of bread and dried dates of poor quality as they had, saying, 'We do not know which of the two carries a greater sin: he who despises what is presented to him or he who despises to present what he possesses.'

The second rule of good conduct is that the visitor should neither suggest nor demand anything in particular, for this may be troublesome for the person visited to produce. If his brother gives him the choice of two foods, let him choose the easiest of the two. It is part of the *Sunna*. And a Tradition relates that the Emissary of God was never offered a choice between two things without choosing the easier.[68]

Al-Aᶜmash related that Abū Wā'il had said, 'I went with a friend of mine to visit Salmān [al-Fārisī] and he presented us with barley bread and coarsely ground salt. My friend said, "If there were some wild thyme in this salt it would be tastier." Salmān went out and pawned his ablution bowl[A] and brought some wild thyme. When we had eaten, my friend said, "Praise be to God who has made us content with what we have been provided." Salmān said, "Had you been content with what had been provided, my ablution bowl would not be in pawn."'

If someone suspects that [suggesting an addition] would be difficult for his brother or that he would dislike it [then he should refrain from doing so]. But if he knows that his brother will be pleased with his suggestion, and that it would be easy for him to perform, then the suggestion is permissible. Al-Shāfiᶜī (may God be pleased with him) did this with al-Zaᶜfarānī while staying with him in Baghdad. Every day al-Zaᶜfarānī would write on a slip of paper the sorts of food to be cooked and would hand it to the slave-girl. One day al-Shāfiᶜī took the slip of paper and added to it another sort of food in his handwriting. When al-Zaᶜfarānī saw this food, he contested it and said: 'I did not order this.' The slave-girl showed him the slip of paper on which there was an addition in al-Shāfiᶜī's hand. When his glance alighted on [al-Shāfiᶜī's] handwriting he was delighted, and he freed the

[A] *Maṭhara* is a vessel used for washing after going to the toilet.

slave-girl because of his joy at al-Shāfiʿī's suggestion.

Abū Bakr al-Kattānī said, 'I entered upon al-Sarī [al-Saqaṭī] and he brought some crumbled bread and began putting half of it in a cup. I said to him, "What are you doing? I can drink it all down in one go." He laughed and said, "This is better for you than going on a pilgrimage."'[A]

One man said, 'Eating is of three kinds: eating with poor persons, where each one gives precedence to the other; eating with cheerful brethren; and eating with men of the world with good manners.'

The third rule of good conduct is that the person visited must feel a longing for his brother who is visiting him; he should solicit suggestions from him so long as he feels that he can act on his suggestion. This is good and has recompense and abundant merit.

The Emissary of God (may God bless him and grant him peace) said, 'He who happens to fulfil the craving [for certain food] of a brother, will have his sins forgiven him. He who has gladdened his believing brother gladdens God (Exalted be He!).'[69] Among the *ḥadīth* narrated by Jābir [ibn ʿAbd Allāh], the Emissary of God said, 'He who has gratified his brother in what he craves, God has written for him a thousand thousand good deeds, erased from him a thousand thousand bad deeds and raised him up a thousand thousand degrees. And God has given him to eat from three gardens: the garden of Paradise, the garden of Eden and the garden of Eternity.'[70]

The fourth rule of good conduct is that [the host] must not say to [the guest] 'Shall I serve you food?' He ought [simply] to serve him if he has any [food]. [Sufyān] al-Thawrī said, 'If your brother visits you, do not say to him "Do you want to eat?" or "Shall I serve you food?" but serve it to him. If he eats, well and good; if not, remove it.'

If a person does not wish to feed [someone] a [certain] food, he

[A] Clearly this was said in jest.

should not show it to him or describe it to him. Al-Thawrī said, 'If you do not wish to feed your children from what you are eating, do not tell them about it and they should not see that you have it.' One of the Sufis said, 'If poor people enter upon you, serve them food; if theologians enter, ask them about some theological problem; if reciters of the Qur'ān enter, show them to the prayer-niche (*miḥrāb*).'

CHAPTER FOUR

The Manners of Hospitality

IT IS CONSIDERED that the manners of hospitality are six [in number]: the invitation, accepting [an invitation], attending, the serving of food, eating and taking leave. Let us, God willing, [now] turn to their explanation.

The Invitation

The Emissary of God (may God bless him and grant him peace) said, 'Do not so go out of your way for a guest that you will come to dislike him, for he who dislikes a guest dislikes God, and he who has disliked God, God has disliked him.'[71] He said, 'There is no good in someone who is not hospitable.'[72] The Emissary of God passed by a man who owned many camels and cattle, but the man did not show him any hospitality. He then came to a woman with some young ewes, and she slaughtered [one] for him. He said, 'Observe the two of them—these traits are solely in the Hand of God. He grants a good disposition to whom He wishes.'[73]

Abū Rāfiᶜ, the freedman of the Emissary of God, said, 'A guest came to stay with the Emissary of God (may God bless him and grant him peace). He said: "Say to such-and-such a Jew that a guest has come to stay with me, and let him lend me flour until the month of Rajab." The Jew replied, "By God, I shall not lend it to him without a pledge." I informed [the Emissary] of this and he said, "By God, I am trustworthy in heaven and trustworthy on earth, and were he to lend it to me I would discharge [the debt]. Take my coat of mail and pledge it with him."'[74]

Whenever Abraham (may God bless him and grant him peace)

wanted to eat, he would walk for a mile or two searching for someone to eat with him.[75] His patronymic was Abu'l-Ḍayfān.[A] [76] Because of the sincerity of his intention in this, his hospitality remains attached to his shrine until today. Not a night passes without a group of three, ten, and up to a hundred people eating there. The servant who looked after the place said that to this day it has not been without a guest for a single night.

The Emissary of God (may God bless him and grant him peace) was asked, 'What is faith?' He said, 'The giving of food and the exchange of greetings.'[77] 'In expiation and grades [of good deeds],' he said, 'the giving of food and the praying by night while people are asleep [is best].'[78] He was asked about the pilgrimage acceptable to God and he said, 'It is the giving of food and of goodly words.'[79] Anas said, 'A house which is not entered by a guest is not entered by angels.'[80] There are countless Traditions about the merit of hospitality and the giving of food, so let us mention the manners pertaining to them.

Regarding the invitation, the host should strive to invite pious and not impious people. In praying for someone who had invited him, the Emissary of God (may God bless him and grant him peace) said, 'May the godly eat your food.'[81] For he said, 'Eat only the food of a pious man and let no one but a pious man eat of your food'[82]—and he had in mind the poor, in particular, rather than the rich. He said, 'The worst food is the food of a banquet to which the rich have been invited in place of the poor.'[83]

In his hospitality, a person must not neglect his relatives, for their neglect creates loneliness and the severing of kinships. He should be careful when inviting friends and acquaintances, for to single out individuals creates loneliness in the hearts of the rest. He should not use his invitation for vainglory or vaunting but for winning over the hearts of the brethren, and for following the *Sunna* of God's Emissary to give food and bring joy to the hearts of believers. He should not invite anyone he knows will find it difficult to accept and who, should he attend, will cause offence

[A] Lit., 'father of guests'.

to those present for any reason. He should only invite those who are happy to accept the invitation.

Sufyān said, 'He who invites to a meal someone averse to accepting has committed a sin; and if the guest [is forced to] accept then [the host] has committed two sins, because he has induced him to eat despite his aversion, and had he known that [he was knowingly being compelled to eat] he would not have eaten.'

Feeding the god-fearing is helping [them] to obey [God], feeding the impious is encouraging impiety. A tailor said to Ibn al-Mubārak, 'I sew the clothes of sultans, so do you fear that I am a supporter of tyrants?' He said, 'The supporters of tyrants are merely those who sell to you the thread and the needle; but you are of the tyrants themselves.'

As regards accepting an invitation, it is a confirmed *Sunna*; the necessity for accepting has been discussed in certain places. The Emissary of God (may God bless him and grant him peace) said, 'Were I invited to eat trotters I would accept, and were I given a leg [of lamb] I would accept.'[84]

[Accepting the Invitation]

There are five ways of observing good manners when accepting invitations. The first is that the rich should not be given preference over the poor in accepting an invitation—for that is arrogance, which is prohibited. Because of this, some have refrained from answering at all, saying, 'To wait for the broth[A] is a humiliation'; while another said, 'When I place my hands in another's dish, my neck is humbled to him.' The arrogant include those who answer the invitations of the rich instead of the poor, and this is contrary to the *Sunna*. The Emissary of God (may God bless him and grant him peace) used to answer the invitation of both the bondsman and the pauper.[85]

Al-Ḥasan ibn ʿAlī (may God be pleased with both of them)

[A] *Maraqa* is the flavoured sauce in which bread is dipped.

passed by some paupers who were begging on the open highway. They had pieces of bread strewn on the sandy ground and were eating. He was on his mule and he greeted them. They said to him, 'Come along and eat, O son of the daughter of the Emissary of God (may God bless him and grant him peace).' He said, 'Yes, God does not like those who are proud.' So he dismounted and sat with them on the ground and ate. Then he gave them salutations and mounted. He said to them, 'I accepted your invitation, so accept mine.' They said, 'Yes.' He set a time and they came. He placed before them the most superb food and sat down to eat with them.

Regarding the words of the man who said 'He in whose bowl I have placed my hand, my neck has been humbled to him,' someone held that this was contrary to the *Sunna*; that it is not so, for he is humbled only if the host is unhappy about his acceptance, and does not take it as an act of kindness nor sees it as a favour to himself from the person invited. The Emissary of God (may God bless him and grant him peace) used to accept invitations when he knew that the host would take it as an act of kindness, an honour, something to be treasured in this world and in the Afterlife. This differs with circumstances, for he who imagines that giving food will be troublesome is doing it only from vainglory or affectation—and it is not part of the *Sunna* to accept such an invitation.[86] It would be more appropriate instead to make one's excuses. Thus one of the Sufis said, 'Accept only the invitation of one who considers that the food [he provides] was destined for you, that he has handed you a charge which you had with him; and who sees that you have done him a favour in accepting that charge from him.'

Sarī al-Saqaṭī said, 'O, for a morsel of food free from wrongdoing [in the eyes of God] and from the favour of any creature!' If the person invited knows that there is no favour in it, he ought not to decline. Abū Turāb al-Nakhshabī said, 'I was offered food and declined, and I was afflicted with hunger for fourteen days. I knew that it was His punishment.' And Maʿrūf al-Karkhī was once told, 'Go to whomever invites you.' He said: 'I am a guest who goes wherever he is invited.'

The second [rule of good conduct] is that a man ought not to decline [an invitation] because of distance or because of the host's poverty or lack of social standing. A distance that can normally be endured should not cause one to abstain. This is why it is said in the Torah or one of the sacred books, 'Walk a mile to visit a sick person, two miles to take part in a funeral, three miles to accept an invitation and four miles to visit a brother in God.' Precedence was given to accepting an invitation and paying a visit because through these one fulfils the right of the living, who are more deserving than the dead.

The Emissary of God (may God bless him and grant him peace) said, 'Were I invited to Kurāᶜ al-Ghamīm, I would accept.' This is a place some miles from Medina where, on his first arrival there in Ramaḍān, the Emissary of God broke the fast and made short his prayers.[87]

The third [rule of good conduct] is that a person should not abstain [from accepting an invitation] because he is fasting but should attend. For if breaking his fast will give pleasure to his brother, then let him break his fast, and let him expect a reward in the Afterlife for having broken his fast with the intention of bringing joy to his brother's heart. This is the same reward he would have obtained for fasting, even better—this being a case of supererogatory fasting. However, if he is not sure that [his brother] would take pleasure [in him breaking his fast], then he should openly tell him [of his intention to do so] and should break his fast. If he becomes certain that [his brother] is [just] pretending [to take pleasure] then he should make an excuse [and not break his fast]. The Emissary of God said to someone who used his fasting as an excuse [for refusing an invitation], 'Your brother has put himself out and you say "I am fasting."'[88]

Ibn ᶜAbbās (may God be pleased with both of them) said, 'The best of good deeds is to treat hospitably those who are seated with you by giving them a meal with which to break the fast. For breaking the fast with such an intention is a form of worship and [proof of] good character; its reward is above that of fasting. The hospitality of someone who is not fasting consists of perfume, the censer[A] and pleasant conversation.' It was said that *koḥl*[B] and oil are two ways to entertain a guest.

The fourth [rule of good conduct] is that one abstain from accepting an invitation if [one knows that] the food is of dubious origin, or that the location or the carpet that is spread out is unlawful, or there is something objectionable in the venue—such as a spread of silk brocade, a silver container, the depiction of an animal on the ceiling or wall, hearing something played on reed and musical instruments, people engaged in some frivolous pastime or making music and listening to calumny and defamation, falsehood, slander, lying and the like. All these things prevent one from accepting an invitation and deeming it desirable. It becomes obligatory to declare [such invitations] unlawful or hateful. The same applies to a host who is tyrannical, heretical, dissolute or evil, who behaves affectedly or is vainglorious and proud.

The fifth [rule of good conduct] is that, by accepting [an invitation], a person should not be intent [solely] on gratifying the appetite of the stomach—as this would be acting for the expedients of this world [alone]. Rather, his intention should be more elevated so that, when he accepts, his aim would be the Afterlife and his intention would be the emulation of the *Sunna* of God's Emissary when he said, 'Were I invited to trotters I would accept.'[89] He should make the intention to be wary of disobedience to God (Exalted be He!), because the Emissary said, 'He who has not accepted the [invitation of] the host has disobeyed God and His Prophet.'[90] He should make the intention to honour his believing brother by following the words of God's Emissary, 'When one honours a believing brother, it is as if one

[A] It is still a common custom in Muslim lands for a host to offer guests a censer of burning incense to perfume their clothes.

[B] Antimony, or *koḥl*, for the eyes and oil for the skin.

had honoured God.'[91] He should make the intention to bring gladness to [his brother's] heart, complying with the Emissary of God's words, 'He who has gladdened a believer has gladdened God.'[92] He should make the intention to visit him, that they may be among those who love one another in God.[93] For the Emissary of God (may God bless him and grant him peace) has stipulated that visits be exchanged and [money] be spent for the sake of God—of the two parties, the spending belongs to him who is paying the visit. He should make the intention to see to it that he is not badly remembered for having declined an invitation, nor that he is defamed for having been prompted by arrogance, bad disposition or disdain for a brother Muslim or things of this nature. These are six intentions. If only one of them affects the correctness of his acceptance as a deed, how about their totality?

One of the *salaf* used to say, 'I prefer to have an intention for every action, even for food, drink and the like.' The Emissary of God (may God bless him and grant him peace) said, 'Actions are [judged] only by [their] intentions and every man shall have that which he intended. Thus he who migrates for God and His Emissary migrates for God and His Emissary; he who migrates for worldly benefit or to take some woman in marriage migrates for whatever he migrates for.'[94] Intentions [to please the brethren] are valid only with permissible actions and pious deeds. But it is not so with prohibited things. If a person intends to gladden his brethren by helping them to drink wine or [to do] some other unlawful thing, the intention would be invalid and it would not be permissible to say that 'actions are [judged] only by [their] intentions.' For example, if his intention in going on a military expedition [for the sake of God], which is a pious act, is self-glorification and the pursuit of wealth, then he will have turned away from pious action. The same applies to all permitted and frequently repeated good deeds and other actions; they are attached to goodness through their intention. So intention affects both these groups but not the third [group].

[Attending an Invitation]
Now, the rules of good conduct with respect to attending [an invitation] require that a person enter the house, but not go to the centre to take the best place. He must be humble. He must not make [the hosts] wait long [before arriving], nor be in such a hurry as to surprise them before they have completed their preparations. He should not make the place too cramped for those present. If the owner indicates a place to him he should certainly not oppose him in that, for [the host] may have set aside in his own mind a place for each person, and contradicting him may upset him. If, in deference to him, [another] guest indicates to him that he should proceed to a higher place he should be modest [and decline]. The Emissary of God (may God bless him and grant him peace) said, 'Being satisfied with an inferior place in the gathering is a way of showing modesty to God.'[95] He should not sit facing the door of the room reserved for the womenfolk, [for this room is intended] to keep them secluded. He should not look too much towards the place whence food is brought, for this is a sign of greed. When he sits down, he ought to single out those close to him for greetings and to inquire about their health.

If a guest who will be spending the night enters, the householder should, on his entering, acquaint him with the *qibla*,[A] the water closet and the place for performing one's ablutions. This is what Mālik [ibn Anas] did with al-Shāfiʿī (may God be pleased with both of them).[B] Mālik washed his hands before the meal and before anyone else did, saying, 'Washing before the meal is more appropriate for the head of the house, for it is he that invites people to his hospitality. Therefore, it is fitting that he should be the first to wash [at the beginning of the meal] and the last to wash at the end of the meal so that he may wait for whoever enters to eat and to eat with him.'

If a person enters and sees something objectionable, he may

[A] The direction which one must face when praying the canonical prayer.
[B] When al-Shāfiʿī visited Medina.

change it if he is able to; otherwise let him express his disapproval verbally[96] and leave. What is objectionable is the spreading of silk brocade, the use of gold and silver dishes, representations [of figures] on the walls, the listening to entertainment and musical instruments, the presence of women with bared faces and other such forbidden things.

Thus Aḥmad [ibn Ḥanbal] (may God have mercy on him) said, 'If one sees a container for *koḥl* whose top is worked with silver, he should leave. He is permitted to sit down only in the presence of a vessel which has been repaired [with silver].'[A] And he said, 'If one sees a diaphanous covering, he should leave, for it is a vain affectation, it repels neither heat nor cold and conceals nothing.' He said that a person should likewise leave if he sees the walls of the house covered with silk brocade, in the same way that the Kaᶜba is covered. He said, 'If a person has rented a house in which there is a picture or enters the bathroom and sees a picture, he should scrape it off, and if he is unable to do so, he should leave.' All that he has mentioned is correct, but merely looking at a diaphanous veil and the ornamentation of walls with brocade does not mean that they are prohibited since only men are forbidden silk. The Emissary of God (may God bless him and grant him peace) said, 'These two are forbidden to the males of my nation but are lawful to its females.'[B] [97] And that which is on walls cannot be attributed to men. If it were forbidden, then the decoration of the Kaᶜba would be forbidden. Rather, it is more befitting that it be allowed, based on God's words: '*Say, who has forbidden the decoration of God?*'[98] And this, especially at times of festivity and if it is envisaged that men will benefit from looking at them; so long as this does not become a custom for the sake of vainglory. It is not forbidden for men to enjoy looking at silk brocade even when worn by slave-girls and women. And walls fall in the same category as women, in that they are not characterised by maleness.

[A] That is, where silver has been used to repair the vessel and the vessel itself is made of some other substance.

[B] In Islam, men are prohibited from wearing silk and gold.

[The presentation of food and eating]

As regarding the presentation of food, there are five rules of good conduct. The first is that the food be served quickly, for this honours the guest. The Emissary of God (may God bless him and grant him peace) said, 'He who believes in God and the Last Day let him be generous to his guest.'[99] When the majority of the guests have arrived, but one or two are absent, being late for the appointed time, those who are present have a greater right to be served quickly than those who are late [have a right] for the meal to be delayed; unless the person who is late is poor or will be greatly distressed by it, in which case there is no harm in delaying. One of the two meanings is found in God's words: '*Has the story of Abraham's honoured guests reached you?*'[100] They were honoured by being served food quickly, as indicated by His words '*and he soon brought a fatted calf*';[101] and his words '*and he hastened to his family and brought a fatted calf.*'[102] It was said that he brought a leg of meat and it was called *ᶜijl* [calf] because he brought it quickly without tarrying.[A]

Ḥātim al-Aṣamm said, 'Haste is from the devil except in five cases of the Emissary's *Sunna*: feeding one's guest, preparing the dead for burial, marrying a virgin, paying back a debt and repenting a sin.'[103] Making haste to a banquet is desirable. It has been said that [a wedding] banquet on the first day is *Sunna*, on the second a courtesy, on the third hypocrisy.'

The second [rule of good conduct] is that, regarding the order of the foods, precedence should first be given to fruit, if there be any, for that is medically fitting. Since fruit is more quickly transmuted,[B] it should lie at the bottom of the stomach. The Qur'ān enjoins the serving of fruit first—in God's words, '*and fruit of their choosing*'[104]; after which He says '*and the meat of birds they desire.*'[105] Thus, the best thing to be served after fruit is meat and *tharīd*.[C] The Emissary of God (may God bless him and grant

[A] The Arabic words for calf and for 'haste' have the same root—*ᶜajala*.

[B] That is, digested.

[C] Flat bread torn into small pieces and soaked in broth along with pieces of meat.

him peace) said, 'The superiority of ᶜĀ'isha over [other] women is like the superiority of *tharīd* over the rest of food.'[106] And if after this a person were brought sweetmeats, [everything] good will have been brought together.

Honouring with meat is indicated in God's words about Abraham, who brought a fatted calf to his guest—namely, calf which has been well cooked. This is one of the two things meant by honouring [a guest], by which I mean serving meat. In His description of good things, God has said: '*We have brought down to you manna and quail.*'[107] Manna is honey and *salwā* [quail] is meat. It was called *salwā*[A] because one takes more pleasure in it than in all the forms of *idām* and nothing can replace it. Thus the Emissary of God (may God bless him and grant him peace) said, 'The chief *idām* is meat.'[108] And after mentioning manna and quails, God said: '*Eat of the good things We have provided you with*'[109]—meat and sweetmeats being among the good things.

Abū Sulaymān al-Dārānī (may God be pleased with him) said, 'Eating good things brings contentment with God.' These good things are completed by drinking cold water and pouring tepid water over the hand when washing. Al-Ma'mūn said, 'Drinking water with ice makes sincere one's thanks to God.'

A man of letters once said, 'If you invite your brethren and feed them *haṣramiyya*[B] and *būrāniyya*[C] and give them cold water to drink, you will have perfected your hospitality.'

One person spent [many] dirhams on hospitality, and a wise man told [him], 'We had no need of this: if your bread is good, your water cold and your vinegar sour, that is enough.' Another said, '[Serving] sweetmeats after the food is better than an abundance of dishes; being comfortable at table is better than increasing [the meal] by two dishes.' It is said that angels are present at a table on which there are vegetables, for that too is

[A] The word *salwā* comes from the same root as the word for being entertained or amused.

[B] A dish made from unripe grapes.

[C] A vegetable stew.

desirable because they are graced with greenness.

Tradition has it that the table which was sent down to the Israelites had on it all the vegetables except leeks; it had on it a fish with vinegar at its head and salt at its tail, and seven loaves of bread with olives and pomegranate seeds on each loaf. When these are brought together, compatibility is achieved.

The third [rule of good conduct] is to serve the choicest dishes first, so that whoever wishes may have his full share of them and not eat too much afterwards. The practice of those who indulge in luxurious living is to serve coarse food first and to rekindle the appetite by offering delicate food only afterwards; this is contrary to the *Sunna*, for it is a device for increasing the intake of food. It used to be the *Sunna* of the people of old to serve all the courses at one and the same time, and to line up the dishes of food on the table for each person to eat of that which he fancied. If [the host] has only one type of food he should mention this, to allow [his guests] their fill of it without having to wait for something better. It is said that a virtuous person used to write out a list of dishes he had asked to be prepared and would show it to his guests. A *shaykh* said, 'A *shaykh* served me a type of food known in Syria and I told him, "In Iraq we serve this only at the end." He said, "It is the same with us in Syria." He had no other sort of food and I was embarrassed for him.'

Another said, 'We were a group at an invitation, and we were presented with various kinds of fried heads, cooked and preserved. We did not eat but waited for some [other] course or a lamb. Then [the host] brought us the basin [to wash our hands after the meal] without anything else being served. We looked at each other and one of the *shaykhs* said in jest, "God (Exalted be He!) is capable of creating heads without bodies." We spent that night hungry and we asked for crumbled bread for *suḥūr*.' It is thus desirable that everything be served [together] or that he notify [his guests] of the kinds of food he has.

The fourth [rule of good conduct] is that a person should not hurry to remove the dishes before [the guests] have had their fill and ceased to eat. For one of them may have found the remainder of that course more appetising than what had previously been presented, or there remained in him a need to eat and he may be put off by the hasty [withdrawal of the food]. This is what is meant by 'being comfortable at table', and it is said to be better than two [more] courses of food. It is likely that the purpose of this is to avoid things being done in a hurry, although it is equally likely that its purpose is to make space [at table].

It is related that al-Sutūrī, a Sufi with a predilection for humour, was present at the table of a worldly man and a lamb was served to them. The man at whose table he ate was somewhat niggardly. When he saw that people had torn the lamb completely to pieces, he was irritated and said, 'Lad, take it to the children.' So the lamb was taken inside the house, but al-Sutūrī, having risen to his feet, ran after the lamb. Someone said to him, 'Where are you going?' He said: 'I'm off to eat with the children.' The man, feeling ashamed, ordered the lamb to be brought back. From this example it is shown that the host should not raise his hand[A] before others have done so, lest they be embarrassed. On the contrary, he should be the last [to stop] eating.

A hospitable man used to inform people of all the dishes [to be served] and to let them have their fill. When they had almost finished, he would squat down and stretch out his hand to the food and eat, saying, 'In the name of God, help me, may God bless you.' The *salaf* found this commendable about him.

The fifth [rule of good conduct] is that a sufficient quantity of food be served, for to serve less indicates lack of good manners. But that to have [food] in excess is affectation and hypocrisy; this is especially so when a person does not intend that [his guests] eat everything. However, if he serves [food] in abundance, and rejoices when people eat it all, his intention being to seek a blessing from the food that remains, then, according to the Tradition, he is not held to account for it.

[A] That is, stop eating.

Ibrāhīm ibn Adham once brought plenty of food to his table and Sufyān [al-Thawrī] said to him, 'O Abū Ishāq, do you not fear that this is extravagant?' Ibrāhīm replied, 'There is no extravagance in food unless the intention is to be extravagant; abundant provision would [then] be an affectation.' Ibn Masʿūd said, 'We have been forbidden to accept the invitation of someone who boasts about his food.' A group of the Companions disliked eating food that had been boasted about.

No leftovers were ever removed from before the Emissary of God (may God bless him and grant him peace), because they used to serve only the necessary quantity, for they did not eat to repletion.

The portion allotted to the members of the household must first be set aside, to prevent their eyes from avidly expecting that some of it will be returned [from the guests]; for maybe it will not be returned and they would feel frustrated and their tongues give vent to feelings against the guests. This would mean that feeding the guests results in [them] being disliked by others and this would be a disloyalty to them.

Whatever remains of the food is not for the guests to take away, but is what the Sufis call *zalla*,[A] unless the person providing the food has clearly and with a consenting heart given [his guests] permission to take it; or this has been understood through indications and circumstances, and he is happy about it. If, however, there is a suspicion that he might be disinclined, then it must not be taken. If his approval is known, fairness and impartiality must be exercised among the company, for none may take more than what pertains to him or that which his companion consents to, willingly rather than through shyness.

[A] The remnants of a meal which are given to the poor. The word *zalla* comes from the root 'to slip or commit an error'. The implication is that the food given away helps expiate sins.

[Taking leave]

There are three rules of good conduct for taking leave. The first is that the host should accompany the guest to the door of the house. This is *Sunna* and a show of respect to the guest, and we have been commanded to show him respect. The Emissary of God (may God bless him and grant him peace) said, 'Let him who believes in God and the Last Day respect his guest.'[110] And he said, 'It is proper behaviour towards a guest that he be accompanied to the door of the house.'[111]

Abū Qatāda said, 'The delegation from the Negus[A] came to the Emissary of God (may God bless him and grant him peace) and he himself served them. His Companions said to him: "There are enough of us to make it unnecessary for you to do this, O Emissary of God." He said: "No, they honoured my Companions and I wish to repay them."'[112]

A full show of respect consists of being of cheerful countenance and pleasant conversation when entering or leaving, and also at table. Al-Awzāʿī was asked, 'What is showing respect to a guest?' He answered, 'A cheerful countenance and pleasant conversation.' Yazīd ibn Abī Zayyād said, 'I never entered upon ʿAbd al-Raḥmān ibn Abī Layla without him conversing with us pleasantly and providing us with good food.'

The second [rule of good conduct] is that the guest make his departure in good spirits, even if he had not been fully treated as is his right—this being a matter of good character and of modesty. The Emissary of God (may God bless him and grant him peace) said, 'A man attains with good character the degree of someone who fasts and who prays at night.'[113]

A messenger was sent to invite one of the *salaf*, but could not find him. When [the man] heard [of the invitation] he went, but everyone had already dispersed, having finished and left.

[A] The Christian king of Abyssinia who gave asylum to a group of early Muslims fleeing persecution in Mecca. When the news that the Negus had died reached the Prophet, he offered the funeral prayer for him.

The owner of the house went out to him and said, 'The people have left.' He said, 'Is there anything left?' The owner said, 'No.' He said, 'A piece of bread only, if there is any left.' The owner said, 'There is nothing left.' He said, 'Then the pot for me to wipe clean.' 'I have washed it,' said the owner. So the man went away giving praise to God. He was asked about that and said, 'The man invited us with good intention and he turned us away with good intention—this is what humility and good disposition mean.'

It is related that a young boy had given his father's invitation to the teacher of Abū Qāsim al-Junayd four times, and [when the teacher of al-Junayd came] the father turned [him] away on the four occasions. On each occasion the latter returned in order to delight the boy's heart by attending and the father's heart by turning [him] away. Such are the souls of those who have effaced themselves in humility to God (Exalted be He!), contented with the belief in the unity of God and who see in every rejection and acceptance an indication of their relationship with their Lord. They are not broken by the humiliation that comes from God's servants, nor do they rejoice in any honour from them. To them everything comes from the One, the Subduer. Thus one of them said, 'I only accept an invitation because it reminds me of the food of Paradise—that is to say, good food that relieves us of toiling for it, supplying it and being made to account for it.'

The third [rule of good conduct] is that he should not go out without the consent and permission of the owner of the house, and he should examine his heart for the amount of time he may stay. If he comes as a guest, his stay should not exceed three days, since [the host] may become bored with him and will need to evict him. The Emissary of God (may God bless him and grant him peace) said, 'Hospitality is for three days; anything more is charity.'[114] Certainly, if the owner were to press him with a sincere heart, he may then stay on. It is desirable that one should have a bed for a guest who is staying.

The Emissary of God (may God bless him and grant him peace) said, 'A bed for the man, a bed for the wife, a bed for the guest—and the fourth is for Satan.'[A] [115]

[A] That is, to have four beds is an extravagance above and beyond all possible needs.

A Section Combining Miscellaneous Good Manners and Legal Prohibitions

ONE: It is related that Ibrāhīm al-Nakhᶜī said, 'To eat in the market is ignoble'—which saying he attributed to the Emissary of God (may God bless him and grant him peace), although the chain of authorities is *gharīb*.[116] A contrary Tradition was transmitted on the authority of Ibn ᶜUmar (may God be pleased with both of them), who said, 'At the time of the Emissary of God (may God bless him and grant him peace), we used to eat while walking and drink while standing up.'[117]

A *shaykh* from among the well-known Sufis was seen eating in the market. Asked about that, he said, 'Woe to you, [do you want me] to be hungry in the market and to eat at home?' He was asked, 'Do you enter the mosque [while eating]?' He answered, 'I am ashamed to enter His house to eat in it.'

The view of the majority is that eating in the market is [a mark of] humility and an abandonment of affectation in some people, in which case it is good; but it is a violation of good manners in others in which case it is reprehensible. It differs according to the customs of the country and to the circumstances of people. Therefore, he who claims that it does not conform to the rest[A] of his actions associates it with a lack of good manners and excessive greed, and so openly censures it. He who finds that abandoning affectation conforms to all his circumstances and

[A] In earlier editions of the *Iḥyā'*, the expression is *sābiq aᶜmālihi*. The sentence hence reads 'his previous actions'. In later editions, the expression is *sā'ir aᶜmālihi* ('the rest of his actions').

actions takes it as a sign of humility.

Two: ʿAlī (may God be pleased with him) said, 'He who starts his meal with salt, God will remove from him seventy kinds of misfortune.[118] He who has eaten seven pressed dates in a day has killed every creature creeping inside his stomach. He who eats twenty-one red raisins every day shall not see anything in his body that he dislikes.'

Flesh makes the flesh grow.[A] *Tharīd* is the food of the Arabs, and *bisqārjāt*[B] enlarges the stomach and makes the buttocks slack. Beef brings disease; cow's milk is a remedy, its clarified butter a medicine; fat removes its like of disease.[C] And a woman in child-bed will find no remedy better than ripe red dates. Fish saps the body, and both reciting the Qur'ān and cleaning the teeth with a tooth-stick [*siwāk*] rid one of sputum. Whoever desires a long life—and life is not long—should take his daytime meal early; let him eat dinner regularly and wear shoes. People will find nothing better for [medical] treatment than clarified butter. One must also reduce the frequency of the sexual act and the incidence of indebtedness.

Three: when al-Hajjāj asked a doctor, 'Prescribe to me something which I can take and no more.' [The doctor] said: 'Do not marry any woman save a young girl; eat only the meat of what is in the prime of life; eat nothing cooked unless it is well done; drink medicine only for a malady; eat only ripe fruit; and do not eat food without chewing it well. Eat the food you like and do not drink on top of it. And if you drink do not eat anything on top of it. Do not withhold your excrement or urine. When you eat during the day go to sleep; when you eat at night walk before you sleep, if only a hundred steps.' These words of the Arabs have the same meaning: 'Take your daytime meal, stretch out; dine, walk'—as God (Exalted be He!) said: '*Then he went to his family walking proudly*.'[119] It is said that to withhold urine ruins the body as the river ruins

[A] Makes one fat.

[B] A kind of stew made of meat and chicken.

[C] It is beneficial against disease.

what is around it when its watercourse is blocked.

Four: the Tradition goes, 'Cutting the blood vessels[A] brings about illness, and giving up the night meal leads to infirmity.'[120] The Arabs say that giving up the night meal does away with the fat of the inner parts of the thighs.

A wise man said to his son, 'O my son, do not go out of your house until you have acquired your powers of discernment—that is, until you have had your day meal,' which keeps discernment and removes rashness. It also lessens one's carnal appetite for whatever one sees in the market.

A wise man said to a fat man, 'I see upon you a velvet cloak of the weaving of your molars, so what is it made of?' He said, 'It is the eating of the best parts of wheat and young goats, and I anoint myself from a long-necked bottle of [water of] violets, and dress myself in linen.'

Five: abstaining from food harms the healthy, while not abstaining harms the ailing.[121] It has been said thus. Someone also uttered, 'He who abstains from certain foods can be certain that nothing adverse shall befall him, is in no doubt about his well-being and is in a sound state of health.'[122]

The Emissary of God (may God bless him and grant him peace) saw Ṣuhayb eating dates when one of his eyes was infected. He asked, 'Do you eat dates when you have an eye infection?' He said, 'O Emissary of God, I eat only on the other side,' meaning on the sound side of his face, and the Emissary of God laughed.[123]

Six: it is desirable that food be taken to the family of a deceased person. When Jaᶜfar ibn Abī Ṭālib's death was announced, [the Emissary of God] said, 'The family of Jaᶜfar are too preoccupied with their dead to prepare their food, so take them something to eat.'[124] And this is *Sunna*. When it is put before the gathering, it is permissible to eat of it, except for what is prepared for the women mourners and female assistants who are weeping and grieving

[A] That is, by being cauterised.

[for the dead person]—this must not be eaten with them.

Seven: a person must not partake of the food of a transgressor. If he is compelled to do so, he must eat little and not seek out the best of the food. One of those examining the suitability of witnesses rejected the testimony of someone who had attended the meal of a sultan, saying, 'I was compelled to do so.' He said, 'I saw you seeking out the best and taking large mouthfuls, and you were not compelled to do that.' The sultan forced the person attesting to [come to] a meal. He said, 'Either I shall eat and give up attesting or I shall attest and not eat.' There was nothing for them to do but to let him be.

It was related that Dhu'l-Nūn al-Miṣrī was imprisoned and did not eat for days while in prison. He had a sister in God who sent him food through the hands of the jailer with [money she made] from her spindle. He abstained and did not eat. The woman reproved him and he said, '[The food] was legitimate but it came to me on the dish of a transgressor'—referring to the hand of the jailer, and this is the acme of piety.

Eight: it is related that Fatḥ al-Mawṣilī had entered upon Bishr al-Ḥāfī as a visitor. Bishr took out a dirham and gave it to Aḥmad al-Jallā', his servant, saying, 'Buy with it some good food and some good condiment.' [His servant] said, 'So, I brought some clean bread,[A] but told myself that the Emissary of God (may God bless him and grant him peace) did not say "Bless us in it and give us increase of it" about anything except milk.[125] So, I bought milk and some good dates, which I presented to him, and he ate and took away what was left over.' Bishr asked, 'Do you know why I said "Buy some good food?" Because good food draws forth sincere thanks [to God]. Do you know why he did not say to me "eat"? Because it is not for the guest to say to the owner of the house "eat". Do you know why he carried off what was left over? Because if one's trust in God is sound, then carrying it off will not do any harm.'

[A] Made from the choicest wheat.

Abū ʿAlī al-Rūdhbāri related that when he entertained he lighted a thousand lanterns. A man said to him, 'You have overdone it,' to which he replied, 'Enter and extinguish everything that I have lit other than to God.' The man entered but was unable to extinguish a single one, and was cut short. Abū ʿAlī al-Rūdhbāri bought some loads of sugar and ordered the sweetmakers to build a wall of sugar on which were battlements and *miḥrāb*s on decorated pillars, all made of sugar. He then invited the Sufis and they destroyed and plundered them.

Nine: al-Shāfiʿī said, 'Eating is of four modes. Eating with one finger is [indicative] of hatred, with two fingers arrogance, with three fingers *Sunna*, with four and five greed.'[126]

Four things strengthen the body: eating meat, inhaling perfume, much washing though no sexual act [was committed] and the wearing of linen.

Four things weaken the body: to partake too frequently of the sexual act, too many worries, too much drinking of water on an empty stomach and too much eating of acid foods.

Four things strengthen the sight: sitting in the direction of the *qibla*, wearing *koḥl* when sleeping, looking at greenery and the cleansing of garments.

Four things weaken the sight: looking at filth, looking at someone crucified, looking at a woman's genitals and sitting with one's back to the *qibla*.

Four things increase one's sexual prowess: eating small birds, truffles, pistachio nuts and watercress.

Sleep is of four kinds: sleeping while leaning on the back of the neck, like the prophets reflecting on the creation of the heavens and the earth; sleeping on one's right side, like scholars and worshippers; sleeping on the left side, like kings, to digest their food; and sleeping on one's front, like the devils.

Four things strengthen the mind: giving up talking about things that do not concern one, [using] a *siwāk* [tooth-stick], sitting in the company of pious men and [sitting in the company of] scholars.

Four things are part of worship: not taking a step without having made one's ablutions, making many prostrations, frequenting mosques and reciting the Qur'ān often.

[Al-Shāfiʿī also] said, 'I am astonished how the person who enters the [steam] bath on an empty stomach, then puts off eating after emerging from it, does not die. And I am astonished how the person who has a cupping, then proceeds to eat, does not die.' He said, 'I have seen nothing more beneficial in an epidemic than [water of] violets with which to anoint oneself and to drink—and God is most knowing about what is correct.'

NOTES

1 Q. XXIII:51.

2 Bukhārī, Waṣāyā, 2742, Nafaqāt, 5354 and Farā'iḍ, 6733, with the wording, 'And there is nothing that you have spent, but that you shall be rewarded for it, even for the morsel of food you raise to the mouth of your wife.'

3 Q. IV:29.

4 This *ḥadīth* appears in the *Musnad* of Qudāᶜī, and is close to the *ḥadīth* in Tirmidhī, Aṭᶜima, 1846 and Abū Dāūd, Aṭᶜima, 3761, 'The blessing of food is the ablution before and after,' generally considered weak.

5 Ibn Ḥanbal, *K. al-Zuhd*, p.21.

6 Bukhārī, Aṭᶜima, 5414, in the words of Anas ibn Mālik, 'The Prophet (may God bless him and grant him peace) ate neither on a *khiwān* nor in a *sukurruja*; and he ate no refined bread. I said to Qatada, 'Then upon what were they wont to eat?' He said, "On a *sufra*."'

7 Al-Ghazālī is referring indirectly to the principle derived from the *ḥadīth* in Muslim, *Jumuᶜa*, 867: 'The worst things [in religion] are those things which are started up [*muhadathāt*], and all innovations in religion [*bidᶜa*] are misguidance.'

8 Bukhārī, Aṭᶜima, 5398.

9 The *ḥadīth*, 'I am but a slave. I sit as a slave sits, and I eat as a slave eats,' appears in Ibn Ḥanbal, *K. al-Zuhd*, p.19 and p.21.

10 Ibn Māja, Aṭᶜima, 3349.

11 *Al-Ghazālī on Disciplining the Soul and Breaking the Two Desires*, trans. T J Winter, Cambridge: The Islamic Texts Society, 1995, pp. 108-164.

12 Bayhaqī, *Shuᶜab al-Īmān*, V. 5869 and ᶜUqaylī, *al-Ḍuᶜafā' al-Kabīr* III. 28: 'Hold bread in esteem, and part of the esteem accorded to bread is that one should not expect anything with it.' Ibn al-Jawzī included this saying in his collection of fabricated *ḥadīth*.

13 Muslim, Masājid, 557, with the wording, 'If the supper is ready and you have made the call to begin the prayer, begin with the supper.'

14 Abū Dāūd, Aṭᶜima, 3764 and Ibn Māja, Aṭᶜima, 3286, with the wording, 'Gather together over your food, mention the Name of God (Exalted be He!) and you will be blessed in it.'

15 Kharāi'ṭī, *Makārim al-Akhlāq* 142.

16 Bayhaqī, *Shuᶜab al-Īmān*, VII. 9622, with the wording, 'The food

most loved to God is the one over which there are many hands.'

17 Referring to the *ḥadīth*, 'O lad, mention the Name of God, eat with the right hand and eat what is before you.' Bukhārī, Aṭʿima, 5376 and Muslim, Ashriba, 2022.

18 Bukhārī, Aṭʿima, 5458; Muslim, Dhikr, 2734.

19 Cf. note 17 above.

20 We did not find a source for this practice, other than the *ḥadīth* in *Shuʿab al-Īmān*, v. 5951: 'The master of all your condiments is salt,' with the word 'master' carrying the sense of 'crowning touch'.

21 Bukhārī, Aṭʿima, 3563 and Muslim, Ashriba, 2064, with the wording, 'The Prophet (may God bless him and grant him peace) never found fault with any food.'

22 Cf. note 17 above.

23 Tirmidhī relates in Aṭʿima, 1848, a long *ḥadīth*, in which the Prophet first tells ʿIkrāsh b. Dhuʿayb to eat from what is in front of him, 'because it is all one sort.' Then, when a bowl of fruit is presented, he says, 'Eat from wherever you please, for it is not all one sort.' Ibn Ḥibbān classified the same *ḥadīth* as weak.

24 Referring to the *ḥadīth*, 'Blessing [*al-baraka*] descends from the centre of the food, so eat from the circumference, not from the centre,' Tirmidhī, Aṭʿima, 1805. This expresses the idea that the centre is where the food is piled up the highest.

25 Ibn Ḥibbān includes a saying prohibiting the cutting of bread with a knife in his collection of weak *ḥadīth*.

26 Nasā'ī, Ṣiyām, 2243, 'Do not cut meat with a knife, but rather bite it off piece by piece.' Nasā'ī calls this *ḥadīth* 'disreputable' (*munkar*). Abū Dāūd (Aṭʿima, 3778) includes the following *ḥadīth*, 'Do not cut meat with a knife, for that is the practice of foreigners, but rather tear it off...,' about which Abū Dāūd says, 'This *ḥadīth* has no strength.'

27 Cf. note 12 above.

28 Muslim, Ashriba, 2033.

29 Ibn Ḥanbal, Musnad, IV. 2678. Tirmidhī, Ashriba, 1887, relates a sound *ḥadīth* prohibiting blowing into vessels (*al-inā'*).

30 Muslim, Ashriba, 2020.

31 Bayhaqī, *Shuʿab al-Īmān*, v. 6009: 'Drink in sips and do not gulp.' There is no mention of liver ailments.

32 Muslim, Ashriba, 2024, 'The Prophet forbade drinking while standing.' This is the general rule; while Bukhārī, Ashriba, 5617 states, 'The Prophet (may God bless him and grant him peace) drank from the well of Zamzam standing.'

33 Tirmidhī, Ashriba, 1887: 'The Prophet (may God bless him and grant him peace) forbade breathing into what is being drunk.'

34 Tirmidhī, Ashriba, 1885, relates, 'Do not drink in one breath as does a camel, but in a second and third; and mention God's name when you drink and praise God when you have finished.' Some scholars consider part of this *ḥadīth*'s

chain of narration weak.

35 We were unable to find a source for this *ḥadīth*.

36 The version in Bukhārī, Hiba, 2571, related by Anas, reads, 'The Prophet (may God bless him and grant him peace) came to our house and asked to drink. So we milked a ewe we had, added some water from our well and gave it to him. Abū Bakr was on his left, ʿUmar in front of him and a Bedouin on his right. When he finished [drinking], ʿUmar said, 'Here is Abū Bakr,' but [the Prophet] gave [the cup] to the Bedouin instead, saying, 'To the right, to the right! Is it not to the right?' Anas said, 'So this is *Sunna*—*Sunna* thrice over!'

37 Cf. note 31 above.

38 We were unable to find a *ḥadīth* source for this last practice of the Prophet.

39 Abū Dāūd, Aṭʿima, 3845 relates the *ḥadīth*, 'When the Prophet (may God bless him and grant him peace) used to finish eating, he would lick his fingers thrice and say, "If a piece of what anyone of you is eating falls, brush away anything harmful on it and eat it, and do not cast it to the Devil." And he would command us to wipe clean the plate, saying, "None of you knows in which of the food is the blessing [*baraka*]."'

40 We were unable to find a source for this.

41 As for wiping clean the dish, see note 39. We are unable to find a *ḥadīth* recommending drinking the water of the washed plate.

42 Q. II:172.

43 Q. CXII:1 and CVI:1, respectively. Nawawī, in *al-Adhkār*, p. 228, relates a *ḥadīth* on the authority of Jābir: 'Whoever forgets to mention the name of God upon his food should recite [the *sūra*], "Say, God is One," when he finishes.'

44 Abū Dāūd, Aṭʿima, 3854; Ibn Māja, Ṣiyām, 1747.

45 Bayhaqī, *Shuʿab al-Īmān*, v. 5762, with the wording, 'Neither blood nor flesh originating from what is forbidden will enter Heaven; and the Fire is most fitting for every piece of flesh originating from what is unlawful.'

46 Ibn Māja, Aṭʿima, 3322, with the wording: 'He to whom God gives food should say, "O God, bless us in what You have provided us with, and provide us with better yet." And he to whom God gives milk to drink should say, "O God, bless us with it, and increase it for us," for I know of no other food or drink more rewarding than milk.'

47 Tirmidhī, Aṭʿima, 1814; Ibn Māja, Aṭʿima, 3331.

48 Bukhārī, ʿIlm, 95: 'When the Prophet (may God bless him and grant him peace) said something, he would repeat it three times to make it understood.'

49 Qudāʿī, *Musnad al-shihāb* (ʿIrāqī, II. 7).

50 Tabarānī, *al-Awsaṭ* (ʿIrāqī, II. 8).

51 We were unable to find a source for either phrase in this *ḥadīth*.

52 This expresses what is said in the next *hadīth.*

53 Azdī considered this a weak *ḥadīth* (ʿIrāqī, II. 8).

54 Muslim, Birr, 2569, with the wording, 'I sought food from you but you gave Me no food...'

55 Kharā'iṭī, 135. Ibn Abī Ḥātim calls the *ḥadīth* 'disreputable' (ʿIrāqī, II. 8).

56 Tirmidhī, Birr, 1984, with the wording: 'The Emissary of God (may God bless him and grant him peace) said, "In Paradise there are rooms the outside of which can be seen from the inside and the inside of which can be seen from the outside." Upon this a Bedouin rose and asked, "To whom do these belong?" And [the Emissary] said, "To those whose speech is sound, who provide food for people, who regularly fast and who pray at night when people are asleep."' Also in Kharā'iṭī, 139, with slight variation.

57 Ibn Ḥanbal, Musnad, XII. 22807.

58 Kharā'iṭī, 144, with the distance between each ditch being 'what can be walked in a hundred years.'

59 Q. XXXIII:53.

60 Bayhaqī, *Shuʿab al-Īmān*, VII. 9647. 'He who is invited and does not respond has disobeyed God and His Emissary; and he who enters without being invited enters as a thief and leaves as a plunderer.'

61 This may be a reference to the *ḥadīth* in Muslim, Ashriba, 2038, which begins: 'One day or one night, the Emissary of God (may God bless him and grant him peace) went out, and there was Abū Bakr and ʿUmar. He said, "What has brought you both out of your houses at this hour?" They said, "Hunger." He said, "By the One in whose Hand is my soul, the same has brought me out. Rise." So they got up and followed him to the house of one of the Anṣār...'

62 Q. XXIV:61. The verse begins, 'No blame is there upon the blind, the lame, the sick, or upon yourselves if you eat from your houses, or the houses of your fathers, or of your mothers, or brothers, or sisters or your friend.'

63 This is perhaps a version of the *ḥadīth* in Bukhārī, Zakāt, 1495 and Muslim, Zakāt, 1074. There is no mention in this version, however, that the Prophet had entered the house of Burayra, ʿĀ'isha's servant. Rather, upon being given the meat from Burayra to give away in charity, he said, 'For her it is charity, and for us a gift.'

64 Makkī, *Qūt al-Qulūb*, II. 313, the questioner is Hāshim al-Awqas.

65 Cf. note 62.

66 The same passage which occurs in *Qūt*, II. 311 identifies the ascetic as Samīr Abū ʿĀṣim.

67 Bayhaqī, *Shuʿab al-Īmān*, II. 960.

68 Bukhārī, Manāqib, 3560; Muslim, Faḍā'il, 2327, with the wording, 'between two matters, except that he chose the easier, as long as it was not a sin.'

69 No reference was found for this *ḥadīth*.

70 ᶜUqaylī, al-Ḍuᶜafā', IV. 29, where he calls it 'an absolutely false *ḥadīth* with no source'.

71 Bayhaqī, *Shuᶜab al-Īmān* VII, 960

72 Ibn Ḥanbal, Musnad, IX. 16778; Kharā'iṭī, 134.

73 Bayhaqī, *Shuᶜab al-Īmān*, VII. 9597: 'The Prophet (may God bless him and grant him peace) passed by a man with a number of camels—sixty, seventy or even a hundred—and cattle and sheep, but who neither invited him to stay nor showed him any hospitality. And he passed by a woman who had some ewes, and she invited him to stay and sacrificed one for him. Then he said, "Look at that one who had such an abundance of camels, cattle, and sheep: we passed by him, but he neither invited us to stay nor showed us any hospitality, and look at this woman who had but some ewes, and yet invited us to stay and sacrificed one for us! Truly such character is in the Hand of God and He grants beauty of character to whom He will."'

74 We were unable to find a source for this *hadith*.

75 Bayhaqī, *Shuᶜab al-Īmān*, VII. 9619.

76 Bayhaqī, *Shuᶜab al-Īmān*, VII. 9617.

77 Bukhārī, Īmān, 12; Muslim, Īmān, 39; Nasā'ī, Īmān, 5000; Abū Dāūd, Ādāb, 5194; Ibn Māja, Aṭᶜima, 3253. In all these sources, the wording is, 'A man asked the Emissary of God (may God bless him and grant him peace), "Which Islam is best?" He answered, "Giving food and greeting those you know and those you do not know."'

78 Part of a long *ḥadīth* in Tirmidhī, Tafsīr al-Qur'ān, 3233.

79 Ibn Ḥanbal, Musnad, V. 14055, with the wording: 'They asked, "What pilgrimage is acceptable to God?" He answered, "It is the giving of food and greetings of peace.'

80 We could not find a source for this *ḥadīth*. ᶜIrāqī gives no source.

81 Cf. note 44 above.

82 This is possibly a variation of the *ḥadīth* in Tirmidhī, Zuhd, 2395 and Abū Dāūd, Ādāb, 4832: 'Take none but a believer as your companion, and let no one but a God-fearing person eat your food.'

83 Bukhārī, Nikāḥ, 5177; Muslim, Nikāḥ, 1432, with the wording, 'The worst food is that of a banquet to which the rich are invited but not the poor; and whoever avoids inviting [people] has disobeyed God and His Emissary.'

84 Bukhārī, Nikāḥ, 5178, with the wording 'and were I to be given trotters, I would accept.'

85 Tirmidhī, Janā'iz, 1017 and Ibn Māja, Zuhd, 4178, with slight variations in the wording.

86 Abū Dāūd, Aṭᶜima, 3754: 'Ibn ᶜAbbās used to say that the Emissary of God (may God bless him and grant him peace) forbade eating the food of those who vie with each other in ostentation.'

87 Muslim, Ṣiyām, 1114, in the

ḥadīth beginning, 'The Emissary of God (may God bless him and grant him peace) set out for Mecca in the Year of the Conquest. It was Ramaḍān, and he fasted until he reached Kurāᶜ al-Ghamīm.'

88 This is perhaps a version of a narration in Bayhaqī, *Shuᶜab al-Īmān*, 3951: 'Some people invited a man to food and he said, "I am fasting." They said, "Break your fast today and fast tomorrow."'

89 Cf. note 84.

90 Muslim, Nikāh, 1432, with the wording, 'He who has not accepted an invitation.'

91 Cf. note 92.

92 This saying and the previous one are included in ᶜUqaylī, IV. 29.

93 This refers to the well-known *ḥadīth* which mentions, among the seven 'whom God will shade with His shade on the Day when there is no shade but His,' 'two men who love each other for the sake of God, so that their meeting each other and taking leave from each other is for Him.' Bukhārī, Ādhān, 660; Muslim, Zakāt, 1031.

94 Bukhārī, Bad' al-Waḥy, 1; Muslim, ᶜImāra, 1907.

95 Bayhaqī, *Shuᶜab al-Īmān*, VI. 8239, with the wording, 'Verily, humility towards Almighty God is satisfied by sitting in an inferior place rather than an honoured one in a gathering.'

96 This echoes a *ḥadīth* in Tirmidhī, Fitan, 2172, and elsewhere: 'Whosoever of you sees something reprehensible (*munkar*), let him change it with his hand. If he is not able to do so, then with his tongue; if he is not able to do so, then with his heart—and that is the weakest of faith.'

97 Nasā'ī, Zīna, 5144, with the wording 'The Prophet (may God bless him and grant him peace) took some silk and held it in his right hand, and took some gold and held it in his left hand, and said, "Verily, these two are forbidden to the males of my community."'

98 Q. VII:32.

99 Bukhārī, Ādāb, 6019; Muslim, Īmān, 47.

100 Q. LI:24.

101 Q. XI:69.

102 Q. LI:26.

103 The saying echoes two *ḥadīth*, both questionable. The first appears in Tirmidhī, Birr, 2012: 'Slowness is from God and haste from the Devil.' The second is in Abū Dāūd, Ādāb, 4810: 'Slowness in all things except in working for the Next Life.'

104 Q. LVI:20.

105 Q. LVI:21.

106 Bukhārī, Aṭᶜima, 5419; Muslim, Faḍā'il al-Ṣaḥāba, 2446.

107 Q. II:57.

108 Bayhaqī, *Shuᶜab al-Īmān*, V. 5902.

109 Q. II:57.

110 Cf. note 91 above.

111 Ibn Māja, Aṭᶜima, 3349.

112 We were unable to find a source for this *ḥadīth*.

113 Ibn Ḥanbal, Musnad, XII. 14055; also Abū Dāūd, Ādāb, 4798

114 Bukhārī, Ādāb, 6019 and Muslim, Luqma, 48.

115 Abū Dāūd, Libās, 4142; also Muslim, Libās, 2084, with the wording, 'A bed for the man, a bed for *his* wife.'

116 ʿIrāqī attributes this to Ṭabarānī and calls it weak, (ʿIrāqī, II. 7).

117 Tirmidhī, Ashriba, 1881.

118 The first part of this saying is found in Bayhaqī, *Shuʿab al-Īmān*, V. 5952.

119 Q. LXXV:33. The *Tafsīr al-Qurṭubī* asserts that the verb *yatamaṭṭā*—'to go proudly'—is a variation of *yatamadda*, 'to go stretched out.'

120 This is actually two separate *ḥadīth* which Ghazālī has combined. 'Giving up the night meal leads to infirmity' is in Tirmidhī, Aṭʿima, 1857. ʿIrāqī considers both *ḥadīth* to be weak.

121 An allusion to a quotation often consider to be *ḥadīth*, 'The stomach is the place of [all] sickness and abstinence is the best of medicine.' ʿIrāqī gives no reference to it; Ibn Abī Dunyā quotes it as a *ḥadīth* in *Kitāb al-Samṭ* as does Ibn Qayyim al-Jawziyya in *Zād al-Maʿād*. Perhaps the *ḥadīth* that is closest to it is, 'The worst container that a man fills is his stomach;' Tirmidhī, Zuhd, 2380, Ibn Māja, Aṭʿima, 3349.

122 Some attribute this saying to Luqmān, the sage referred to in Q. XXXI.

123 Ibn Māja, Ṭibb, 3443, with the wording, 'I came up to the Emissary of God (may God bless him and grant him peace) and I had bread in one hand and a date in the other. He said, "Go ahead and eat," so I began to eat. He said, "You are eating dates when you have an eye infection." I said, "Yes, but I'm swallowing from the other side," at which the Emissary of God (may God bless him and grant him peace) smiled.'

124 Ibn Māja, Janā'iz, 1599.

125 Cf. note 46 above.

126 For the *Sunna* of eating with three fingers, see Muslim, Ashriba, 2032.

APPENDIX

PERSONS CITED IN THE TEXT — EXCLUDING PROPHETS

ᶜABD ALLĀH IBN AL-MUBĀRAK, ibn Wāḍiḥ al-Ḥanẓalī (d. 181[797-8])—14,31. An influential saint and scholar of the Law. Originally from Merv in Central Asia, he travelled to study with Mālik ibn Anas in Medina and al-Awzāᶜī in Syria before he died in combat against the Byzantines. His works on renunciation and the Holy War have been published and are still popular. (GALS, I. 256; Ṣafadī, XVII. 419-201; Abū Nuᶜaym, *Ḥilya*, VIII. 162-91; ᶜAṭṭār, 124-8.)

ABŪ ᶜALĪ AL-RŪDHBĀRĪ (d. 322 [933/4])—51. The well-known Sufi of Baghdad, who also spent time in Egypt. He was associated with the circle of al-Junayd and al-Nūrī. He was also a *ḥadīth* scholar and jurist who studied under Ibrāhīm al-Ḥarbī. (Qushayrī, I. 162; Sulamī, 362-9; *Tārīkh Baghdād*, I. 329-33.)

ABŪ AYYŪB AL-ANṢĀRĪ, Khālid ibn Zayd al-Najjārī (d. c 52 [672])—21. One of the first Medinese Muslims, present at the first 'Pledge of al-ᶜAqaba' and host to the Prophet before the Prophet had constructed his house. In later years he was governor of Medina under the Caliph ᶜAlī, and died during a siege of Constantinople. His tomb remains to this day the spiritual hub of Istanbul. (*EI*[2] I. 108-9 [E. Lévi-Provençal et al.]; *Iṣāba*, I. 404-5.)

ABŪ BAKR AL-ṢIDDĪQ ibn Abī Quḥāfa al-Taymī (d. 13 [634])—9, 21. A small businessman of Mecca who personally accompanied the Prophet on his emigration to Medina, Abū Bakr became the Prophet's closest advisor, and after his death became the first caliph. His short reign (11/632-13/634) saw the quelling of an uprising in Central Arabia and the beginnings of the conquest of Iraq and Palestine. (*EI*[2], I. 109-11 [W. Montgomery Watt].)

ABU'L-HAYTHAM, Mālik ibn al-Tayyihān al-Anṣārī al-Awsī (d. 20 [641])—21. One of the first two Anṣār to embrace Islam in Mecca, the other being Asᶜad ibn Zirāra. Abū'l-Haytham is said to have been a poet, and among those opposed to idol worship even during the jāhiliyya. He died during the Caliphate of ᶜUmar, or according to others, of ᶜAlī. (Al-Aᶜlām, v. 208.)

ABŪ QATĀDA, al-Ḥārith ibn Rabīᶜ (d. 54 [673/4])—43. One of the Anṣārī Companions. He lived in Medina and died in Kūfa. About fifty of the *ḥadīth* he transmitted figure in Bukhārī and thirty in Muslim. (Abū Nuᶜaym, *Ḥilya*, VI. 336.)

ABŪ RĀFIᶜ, Aslam Mawlā Rasūl Allāh (d. 35 [655])—29. Born in Medina, Abū Rāfiᶜ was originally the slave of ᶜAbbās ibn ᶜAbd al-Muṭṭalib, who gave him as a gift to the Prophet, who then freed him. His conversion to Islam is said to have taken place before the battle of Badr, and he took part in the Battle of Uḥud. He narrated *ḥadīth* directly from the Prophet and from ᶜAbd Allāh ibn Masᶜūd. He died in Medina slightly before or after the beginning of ᶜUthmān's Caliphate. (*Iṣāba*, V. 65.)

ABŪ SULAYMĀN AL-DĀRĀNĪ, ᶜAbd al-Raḥmān (d. 205 [820/1] or 215 [830/1])—39. Well-known to the Sufis for his piety and renunciation, he was responsible for characteristic maxims like 'The heart is ruined when fear departs from it even for one moment', and 'The sign of perdition is the drying-up of tears'. (Qushayrī, I. 96-8; Sulamī, 68-73; Hujwīrī, 112-13; Abū Nuᶜaym, *Ḥilya*, IX. 254-80.)

ABŪ TURĀB AL-NAKHSHABĪ, ᶜAskar ibn Muḥammad ibn Ḥusayn (d. 245 [859])—32. A renowned shaykh from Khurāsān, contemporary of Ḥātim al-Aṣamm al-Balkhī and transmitter of many *ḥadīth*. One of his oft-quoted sayings: 'O people! You love three things which do not belong to you. You love the self, yet it belongs to God [or in some versions, "to its desires"]; you love the spirit, yet it belongs to God; and you love wealth, yet it belongs to the inheritors. And you seek two things, but find none: comfort and happiness—for they are in Heaven.' (Sulamī, 146-151; Abū Nuᶜaym, *Ḥilya*, X. 219.)

ABŪ WĀ'IL, Shaqīq ibn Salama (d. 82 [702])—25. One of the greatest of the *tābiᶜūn*. He was alive in the Prophet's lifetime, but did not meet him. He figures as the second narrator in over 150 *ḥadīth* in Bukhārī and about 80 in Muslim, reporting from ᶜĀ'isha, renowned Companions and Ibn Masᶜūd. He died during the caliphate of ᶜUmar ibn ᶜAbd al-ᶜAzīz. (Abū Nuᶜaym, *Ḥilya*, IV. 103; Sulamī, 201.)

AḤMAD IBN ḤANBAL (d. 241 [855])—37. The great *ḥadīth* scholar after whom the Ḥanbalī school of law is named. He travelled extensively in search of Traditions, of which he is said to have committed over three hundred thousand to memory. A companion of Bishr al-Ḥāfī and Maᶜrūf al-Karkhī, he was held in high regard by the Sufis, who attribute a number of miracles to him. His tomb is one of the most frequented centres of pilgrimage in Baghdad. (*EI²*, I. 272-7 [H. Laoust]; Abū Nuᶜaym, *Ḥilya*, IX. 161-234; Hujwīrī, 117-8.)

AḤMAD AL-JALLĀ', Abū 'Abd Allāh ibn Yahyā (d. 250 [864-5])—50. A celebrated master from Syria and companion of Abū Turāb and Dhū'l-Nūn. Among his sayings is, 'He for whom praise and blame are equal is an ascetic [*zāhid*]; he who fulfils what is obligatory on time is a devotee [*ᶜābid*]; he who regards all actions as issuing from God and sees naught but One is a unitarian [*muwāḥḥid*].' (Qushayrī, I. 125-6.)

ᶜĀ'ISHA bint Abī Bakr (d. 58 [678])—XI, XIII, 39. The third and most beloved wife of the Prophet. During his final illness he asked his other wives for leave to stay in her house, where he died. After his death she was involved in the revolt of Ṭalḥa and al-Zubayr against the Caliph ᶜAlī, after which she lived quietly at Medina until she died. She was well-versed in Arab history and in poetry, and some of her verses have been preserved. (*EI*², I. 307-8 [W. Montgomery Watt].)

ᶜALĪ IBN ABĪ ṬĀLIB (d. 40 [660])—5, 20, 24, 48. The cousin and son-in-law of the Prophet, having married his daughter Fāṭima. He was usually the Prophet's standard-bearer on expeditions, and became the model of the Muslim knight for later generations. He lived a life of austerity and piety. Upon the death of ᶜUthmān (35/656) he accepted, with some reluctance, the office of caliph, which he held for five years punctuated by several rebellions, including that of Muᶜāwiya, the governor of Syria. He was assassinated at Kūfa by a member of the extreme Khārijite sect, which repudiated him for having agreed to negotiate with Muᶜāwiya. (*EI*², I. 381-6 [L. Veccia Vaglieri]; *Istīᶜāb*, III. 26-67.)

AL-AᶜMASH, Sulaymān ibn Mihrān al-Asadī (d. 147 [764/5])—25. A Qur'ān specialist of Persian origin who studied under Mujāhid at Kūfa. One of the fourteen readings of the Qur'ān bears his name. In addition, Sufyān al-Thawrī and Ibn ᶜUyayna both studied *ḥadīth* under him.' (Azami, 101-2, *Tārīkh Baghdād*, IX. 3-13; *Mashāhīr*, 111; *EI*², I. 431 [C. Brockelmann-Ch. Pellat].)

ANAS ibn Mālik ibn al-Naḍr (d. between 91-3 [709/10-711/12])—4, 7, 15, 24, 30. A celebrated Companion of the Prophet. His mother presented him, at an early age, to the Prophet in fulfilment of a vow. After the Prophet's death he participated in the wars of conquest. One hundred and twenty-eight Traditions on his authority are found in Bukhārī and Muslim. (*Iṣāba*, I. 84-5; *EI*², I. 482 [A. J. Wensinck-J. Robson].)

ᶜAWN, ibn ᶜAbd Allāh al-Masᶜūdī (d. c 115 [733])—21. Member of the *tābiᶜūn* generation, a preacher, poet and narrator of *ḥadīth*. He was a noted host among the people of Medina, then lived in Kūfa where he was known for his devotion and recitations. He also kept company with ʿUmar ibn ʿAbd al-ʿAzīz during his caliphate. Among his many sayings on the remembrance of God, 'If there came over people an hour in which God was not invoked, everyone on earth would be utterly destroyed.' (Abū Nuʿaym, *Ḥilya*, IV. 261; Al-Aʿlām, V. 98.)

AL-AWZĀʿĪ, 'Abd al-Raḥmān ibn ʿAmr (d. 157 [774])—XIII, 43. The principal Syrian authority on the *sharīʿa* of his generation, he placed special emphasis on the 'living tradition' of the Muslim community as an authoritative source of law. His *madhhab* also spread to North Africa and Spain, where it was later replaced by that of Mālik. His tomb near Beirut is still visited. (*EI^2*, I. 772-73 [J. Schacht]; GALS, I. 308-9; Fihrist, 227.)

BISHR IBN AL-ḤĀRITH 'al-Ḥāfī' (d. c 227 [841/2])—50. One of the most celebrated figures of early Sufism, he was a companion of Fuḍayl ibn ʿIyāḍ. Formerly given to riotous living, his repentance is said to have come when, in a state of inebriation, he picked up a scrap of paper on which was written the name of God, which he perfumed and put in a clean place. That night he received a dream in which God told him that He would perfume his name as a reward for his act. Many other tales of his charismatic and devout life have found their way into the classical works on Sufism. (Qushayrī I. 73-7; Hujwīrī 105-6; Abū Nuʿaym, *Ḥilya*, VIII. 336-60; Sulamī, 33-40; *EI^2*, I. 1244-46 [F. Meier]; Dermenghem, 67-78.)

BURAYRA (dates unknown)—22. Originally, Burayra was a slave who came to ʿĀ'isha wanting to serve her. On the Prophet's advice, ʿĀ'isha asked to buy her freedom from her owners—who consented, on the condition that they could retain guardianship (*walā'*) over her, giving them control over whom she could marry in the future. According to some versions, the Prophet mounted the *minbar* in the mosque and said, 'What is wrong with people who create conditions that are not in the Book of God? Anyone who makes such a condition, has nothing were he to make it a hundred times.' Thereupon, Burayra was manumitted unconditionally and became ʿĀ'isha's maidservant. (*Iṣāba*, VIII. 28)

DHU'L-NŪN al-Miṣrī, Thawbān (d. 245 [859/60])—50. Born in Upper Egypt, he travelled to Mecca and Damascus, and became a leading exponent of Sufism. It is said that he was the first to give a systematic explanation of the *aḥwāl* ('states') and *maqāmāt* ('stations') encountered on the spiritual path. A number of miracles are attributed to him, as well as some fine poetry. (*EI^2*, II. 242 [M. Smith]; Sulamī, 23-32; Qushayrī, I. 58-61; Hujwīrī 100-3; Massignon, *Essai*, 206-13.)

[AL-]FUḌAYL ibn ʿIyāḍ (d. 187 [803/4])—23. A brigand who repented and became a pioneer of early Sufism. He studied *ḥadīth* under Sufyān al-Thawrī and Abū Ḥanīfa, and became well-known for his sermons on the worthlessness of the world, which he likened to 'a madhouse where the people are lunatics wearing the shackles of desire and sin.' (Hujwīrī, 97-100; Sulamī, 7-12; Mashāhīr, 149; *EI²*, II. 936 [M. Smith]; GAS, I. 636; Dermenghem, 51-66.)

AL-ḤAJJĀJ, ibn Yūsuf al-Thaqafī (d. 95 [714])—48. An Umayyad general notorious for his ruthlessness. Of humble origins, he was born near al-Ṭā'if, and joined the Damascene police. He attracted the attention of the Caliph ʿAbd al-Malik, who put him in charge of a campaign against Ibn al-Zubayr, whom he defeated and killed at Mecca. He also fought extensively against the Khārijites. (*EI²*, III. 39-43 [A. Dietrich.])

HĀRŪN AL-RASHĪD (regn. 170-193 [786-809])—15. Perhaps the best-known ʿAbbāsid caliph, whose cultured and sumptuous court nevertheless presided over an empire troubled by rebellion and Byzantine encroachments.

AL-ḤASAN al-Baṣrī (d. 110 [728/9])—19,22,23. Perhaps the best known personality among the second generation of Muslims, he was born in Medina and took part in the conquest of eastern Iran. He then moved to Basra, where his sanctity and great eloquence attracted great numbers to his circle. He was also a judge and authority on *ḥadīth*. His tomb at Basra remains an important centre for devout visits. (Hujwīrī 86-7; Abū Nuʿaym, *Ḥilya*, II. 131-61; ʿAṭṭār, 19-26; *EI²*, III. 247-8 [H. Ritter].)

AL-ḤASAN IBN ʿALĪ (d. c 50 [670/1])—14, 31. Grandson of the Prophet and second Imām of the Shīʿa. Until the reign of ʿAlī he lived a secluded life at Medina, interrupted briefly when he claimed the Caliphate. (*EI²*, III. 240-43 [L. Veccia Vaglieri].)

ḤĀTIM AL-AṢAMM al-Balkhī (d. 237 [851/2])—38. A disciple of the Khurāsānī Sufi Shaqīq al-Balkhī, he was known as the 'Luqmān of this nation' for his wise sayings. (Hujwīrī 115; Ṣafadī, XI. 233-4; Sulamī, 80-87; Abū Nuʿaym, *Ḥilya*, XIII. 73-84.)

HISHĀM—22. Unidentified. The version in Qūt al-Qulūb identifies the questioner as Hāshim al-ʿAwqas, also unidentifed.

IBN ʿABBĀS, ʿAbd Allāh (d. 68 [687/8])—XIII, XV, 33. A cousin and close companion of the Prophet respected for his piety and commonly acknowledged as the greatest scholar of the first generation of Muslims. He was a narrator of *ḥadīth* and the founder of the science of Qur'ānic exegesis. He fought alongside ʿAlī at Ṣiffīn, and died at al-Ṭā'if, where the site of his grave is still visited. (Nawawī, Tahdhīb, 351-54; Abū Nuʿaym, *Ḥilya*, I. 314-29; Mashāhīr 9; *Iṣāba*, II. 322-26; *EI²*, I. 40-41 [L. Veccia Vaglieri].)

IBN ABĪ LAYLA, ʿAbd al-Raḥmān Abū ʿĪsā (d. 83 [702])—43. One of the *tābiʿūn*, he lived in Kūfa and died in Dārayā, a village close to Damascus. He figures in the transmission of scores of *ḥadīth*. (Abū Nuʿaym, *Ḥilya*, IV. 354.)

IBN MASʿŪD, ʿAbd Allāh al-Hudhalī (d. between 32-3 [652/3-653/4])—15, 42. Of Bedouin origin, Ibn Masʿūd is said to have been either the third or the sixth convert to Islam; he was particularly well-versed in the recitation and interpretation of the Qur'ān, and was an expert in matters of law. In addition, he related a number of the most important eschatological *ḥadīth*. (*EI²*, III. 873-5 [J.-C. Vadet]; *Iṣāba*, II. 360-62; *Istīʿāb*, II. 308-16.)

IBN SHAYBĀN, Ibrāhīm al-Qirmīsīnī. (d. c. 290 [904])—6. Companion of Ibrāhīm al-Khawwās. Among his many sayings: 'God has given to the believers two things in this world in place of two things they will have in the next. Instead of Heaven, He has given them mosques in which to sit, and instead of the vision of His Face, He has given them the vision of their brethren's faces.' (Sulamī, 402; Abū Nuʿaym, *Ḥilya*, X. 43.)

IBN ʿUMAR, ʿAbd Allāh (d. 73 [693/4])—7, 20, 47. A Companion of the Prophet who, at the age of fourteen, asked to be permitted to fight at Uḥud, which was denied. He possessed high moral qualities, and commanded universal deference and respect. Although it is said that he was offered the caliphate on three separate occasions, he kept himself aloof from politics and occupied himself instead with study and instruction. (*EI²*, I. 53-4 [L. Veccia Vaglieri]; *Iṣāba*, II. 338-41; Abū Nuʿaym, *Ḥilya*, I. 292-314.)

IBRĀHĪM IBN ADHAM (d. c. 160 [776/7])—6, 42. One of the most prominent early Sufis. According to the traditional account, he was a prince of Balkh in Afghanistan who renounced his kingdom to search for God. It is said that he studied under the great jurist Abū Ḥanīfa. He died during a naval expedition against the Byzantines. (*EI²*, III. 985-6 [Russell Jones]; Qushayrī, I. 54-7; Hujwīrī, 103-5; Sulamī, 13-22; Abū Nuʿaym, *Ḥilya*, VII. 367-95, VIII. 3-58.)

JĀBIR ibn ʿAbd Allāh al-Khazrajī al-Anṣārī (d. between 68-78 [687/8-697/8])—24, 26. A Companion of the Prophet whose father died at the battle of Uḥud. He participated in nineteen expeditions of the Prophet, and related a sizeable number of Traditions. (*Iṣāba*, I. 214-15; Nawawī, *Tahdhīb*, 184-6; *Mashāhīr*, 11.)

JAʿFAR ibn Abī Ṭālib (d. 8 [629])—49. A cousin of the Prophet and the elder brother of ʿAlī. It was he that led the emigration to Abyssinia, whence he returned for the Khaybar expedition (7/628). He was known as 'Abu'l

Masākīn' because of his concern for the poor. (*EI*², II. 372 [L. Veccia Vaglieri]; *Istīʿāb*, I. 211-4.)

JAʿFAR IBN MUḤAMMAD ibn ʿAlī ibn al-Ḥusayn, 'al-Ṣādiq' (d. 148 [765])—14, 19. A major authority on law and *ḥadīth*, he taught both Abū Ḥanīfa and Mālik. His austere and saintly life made him an important ideal for the Sufis, who gathered large numbers of sayings attributed to him. He was later made into the seventh Imam of the Shīʿa—the Jaʿfariyya sect is named after him. (*EI*², II. 374-75; [M.G.S. Hodgson]; *Mashāhīr*, 127; Abū Nuʿaym, *Ḥilya*, III. 192-206; *Tahdhīb al-Tahdhīb*, II. 104.)

AL-JUNAYD, Abū'l-Qāsim ibn Muḥammad (d. 298 [910/11])—44. The best known of the Sufis of Baghdad. A nephew and disciple of al-Sarī al-Saqaṭī, he vowed that he would not teach during the latter's lifetime out of deference to his preceptor; however he received a vision of the Prophet, who told him that 'God shall make your words the salvation of a multitude of mankind'; he then began to teach. His gatherings 'were attended by jurists and philosophers [attracted by his precise reasoning], theologians [drawn by his orthodoxy] and Sufis [for his discourse on the Truth].' In addition, he was an authority on theology and law, in which he followed the school of Abū Thawr. (Sulamī, 141-50; GAS, I. 647-50; *EI*², II. 600 [A. J. Arberry]; A. H. Abdel-Kader, *The Life, Personality and Writings of al-Junayd*.)

AL-KATTĀNĪ, Muḥammad ibn ʿAlī Abū Bakr (d. 322 [933/4])—26. A Baghdad Sufi of the circle of al-Junayd and al-Kharrāz. He spent much of his life in Mecca, where he died. (Sulamī, 386-91; *Tārīkh Baghdād*, III. 74-6; Abū Nuʿaym, *Ḥilya*, X. 357-8; ʿAṭṭār, 253-6.)

MĀLIK IBN ANAS, al-Aṣbaḥī (d. 179 [795/6])—16, 36. The founder of one of the four main schools of Islamic law. Born into a family of *ḥadīth* scholars at Medina, he studied the recitation of the Qur'ān with Nāfiʿ and heard *ḥadīth* from al-Zuhrī and Ibn al-Munkadir. He taught al-Shāfiʿī, al-Thawrī and Ibn al-Mubārak. His book, the *Muwaṭṭa'*, is the earliest surviving work of Muslim law, and places great emphasis on the actual practice of Islam in Medina in Mālik's time. (*SEI*, 320-4 [J. Schacht])

AL-MA'MŪN (regn. 198-218 [813-833])—39. The caliph who presided over the zenith of Abbasid civilisation. He led a number of successful campaigns against the Byzantines and provincial rebels. His adoption of Muʿtazilite theology may have been an attempt to reconcile both the Shīʿa and the emerging Sunni orthodoxy to the ruling dynasty.

MAʿRŪF AL-KARKHĪ, ibn Fīrūz (d. 200-1 [815/6-816/7])—32. One of the major early Sufis. His parents are said to have been Christians. He was a major influence on al-Sarī al-Saqaṭī, but also instructed Ibn Ḥanbal in *ḥadīth*. His grave, restored in 1312 AH, is an important focus of the religious life of Baghdad, and many miraculous cures are said to be worked there. (Hujwīrī, 113-15; Sulamī, 74-79; Qushayrī, I. 65-8; Ibn al-Jawzī, *Manāqib Maʿrūf al-Karkhī wa-akhbāruhu.*)

AL-MAWṢILĪ, Fath ibn Saʿīd—50. An unidentified Sufi.

MUʿĀWIYA IBN ABĪ SUFYĀN ibn Ḥarb ibn Umayya (regn. 40-60 [661-80])—15. The first caliph of the Umayyad dynasty, able and astute, he continued the conquests of his predecessors.

MUḤAMMAD IBN WĀSIʿ al-Azdī (d. 127 [744/5])—22. An early *ḥadīth* scholar noted for his asceticism. His statement, 'I never saw anything without seeing God therein' was much discussed by later Sufis. He fought under Qutayba ibn Muslim during the conquest of Transoxiana, and later became a judge. (Hujwīrī, 91-92; Abū Nuʿaym, *Ḥilya*, II. 345-57; *Ghāya*, II. 274; *Mashāhīr*, 151.)

AL-NAKHĪ, Ibrāhīm—47. An unidentified Sufi.

SALMĀN AL-FĀRISĪ (d. 36 [656/7])—XII, XIII, 24, 25. 'Salmān the Good'. A Persian convert to Islam who became one of the most celebrated Companions of the Prophet. It was upon his counsel that the famous 'Fosse' was dug to defend Medina from the Meccan army. He later participated in the conquest of Iraq. His asceticism and devotion to the Prophet made him an ideal for later generations, and in particular the Sufis, to whom he is held to have transmitted much of the Prophet's esoteric knowledge. (*Iṣāba*, II. 60-61; Abū Nuʿaym, *Ḥilya*, I. 185-208; *SEI*, 500-1 [G. Levi della Vida].)

AL-SARĪ AL-SAQAṬĪ, ibn al-Mughallis (d. c 251 [865/6])—26, 32. The maternal uncle of al-Junayd, and one of the first to present Sufism in systematic fashion. According to Hujwīrī, his conversion to Sufism was instigated by the Baghdad saint Ḥabīb al-Rāʿī, who, upon being given a crust of bread by al-Sarī, said, 'May God reward you!' 'From that time on,' al-Saqaṭī later remarked, 'my worldly affairs never prospered again.' He was perhaps the most influential disciple of Maʿrūf al-Karkhī. (*EI²*, IV. 171 [L. Massignon]; *Tārīkh Baghdād*, IX. 187-62; al-Murābiṭ, *al-Sarī al-Saqaṭī*; Dermenghem, 115-28.)

AL-SHĀFIʿĪ, Muḥammad ibn Idrīs al-Qurashī (d. 204 [820])— 16, 25, 26, 36, 51, 52. The founder of the Shāfiʿite school of Islamic law. Although born in Gaza he was brought up with a Bedouin tribe, which gave him a good grounding in poetry and the Arabic language. He later studied *fiqh* with Sufyān ibn ʿUyayna and Mālik ibn Anas, developing a legal theory that stood halfway between literalism and personal opinion. He travelled extensively in Iraq and Egypt, where he died; his tomb today is one of the centres of Cairene religious life. (GAS, I. 484-90; Tārīkh Baghdād, II. 56-73; *SEI*, 512-5 [W. Heffening].)

SUFYĀN AL-THAWRĪ, ibn Saʿīd (d. 161 [777/8])—23, 26, 27, 31, 42. A scholar and well-known saint of Kūfa, about whom a great number of anecdotes are recorded. He was one of the 'Eight Ascetics,' who usually included ʿĀmir ibn ʿAbd Qays, Abū Muslim al-Khawlānī, Uways al-Qaranī, al-Rabīʿ ibn Khuthaym, al-Aswad ibn Yazīd, Masrūq, and al-Ḥasan al-Baṣrī. It is said that he was offered high office under the Umayyads but consistently declined. (*Fihrist*, 225; Abū Nuʿaym, *Ḥilya*, VI. 356-93, VII. 3-144; *EI*, IV. 500-2 [M. Plessner].)

ṢUHAYB ibn Sinān, 'al-Rūmī' (d. c 38 [658/9])—49. An Arab from the Mosul region captured and enslaved as a child by Byzantine raiders. He was brought up in the Byzantine empire, and then taken to Mecca and sold. Here he joined the new Muslim community at the house of al-Arqam, and was persecuted for his faith until he made the Emigration to Medina in the company of ʿAlī. (Ṣafadī, XVI. 335-8; *Iṣāba*, II. 188-9; Abū Nuʿaym, *Ḥilya*, I. 151-6.)

AL-SUTŪRĪ—41. An unidentified Sufi.

THĀBIT AL-BUNĀNĪ, ibn Aslam (d. 127 [744/5])—15. One of the tābiʿūn from Basra who kept company with Anas ibn Mālik for forty years. One of the 'Weepers', he was much given to prayer and other devotional acts. A number of *ḥadīth* are related on his authority. (*Tahdhīb al-Tahdhīb*, II. 2-4; *Mashāhīr*, 89; Abū Nuʿaym, *Ḥilya*, II. 318-33.)

ʿUMAR IBN ʿABD AL-ʿAZĪZ ibn Marwān (regn. 99-101 [717-20])—15. Sometimes called 'the fifth rightly-guided Caliph' for his piety, he was concerned to implement the sharīʿa in a number of neglected areas, such as the equal treatment of converts; he also ended the public cursing of ʿAlī from the pulpits. A large body of sermons and anecdotes connected with him soon found its way into religious literature.

ʿUMAR IBN AL-KHAṬṬĀB (regn. 13-23 [634-44])—9, 21. At first an enemy of the Prophet's mission, he became one of its staunchest defenders. His daughter Ḥafṣa married the Prophet after the Emigration. When he succeeded Abū Bakr as caliph, he showed considerable brilliance in the face of the new circumstances arising as a result of the conquests, regulating the status of minorities, arranging a military pensions system and founding a number of garrison towns (*amṣār*). He was universally respected for his integrity and uncompromising devotion to the faith. (*Iṣāba*, II. 511-12; *Istīʿāb*, II. 450-66;

SEI, 600–1 [G. Levi della Vida].)

YAZĪD IBN ABĪ ZAYYĀD, Abū ʿAbd Allāh (d. 136 [753])—43. One of the *tābiʿūn* from Kūfa he narrated many *ḥadīth* from Ibn Abī Laylā, principally found in Ibn Māja, Abū Dāūd and Tirmidhī. (*Mawsūʿat al-Ḥadīth al-Sharīf*)

AL-ZAʿFARĀNĪ, al-Ḥasan ibn Muḥammad ibn al-Ṣabbāḥ al-Bazzār (d. 259 [873])—25. He was one of Imām Shāfiʿī's principal narrators of *ḥadīth*, known for his eloquence and knowledge of the Arabic language. He died in Baghdād. (*Al-Aʿlām*, II. 212)

Index to Qur'ānic Quotations

SŪRA	VERSE	PAGE
II. *al-Baqara*	172	10
	57	39
IV. *al-Nisā'*	29	3
VII. *al-Aʿrāf*	32	37
XI. *Hūd*	69	38
XXIII. *al-Mu'minūn*	51	2
XXIV. *al-Nūr*	61	22
XXXI. *Luqmān*	102	49
XXXIII. *al-Aḥzāb*	53	21
LI. *al-Dhāriyāt*	24	38
	26	38
LVI. *al-Wāqiʿa*	20	38
	21	38
LXXV. *al-Qiyāma*	33	48
CVI. *Quraysh*	1	11
CXII. *al-Ikhlāṣ*	1	11

BIBLIOGRAPHY

Includes all work cited, with the exception of articles from the *Encyclopaedia of Islam*

ʿAbd al-Bāqī, Muḥammad Fu'ād. *Al-Muʿjam al-Mufahras li alfāẓi al-Qur'ān al-Karīm*. Cairo, 1994.

Abdelkader, A.H. *The Life, Personality and Writings of al-Junayd*. London, 1962.

Arberry, A.J. *Muslim Saints and Mystics. Episodes from the Tadhkirat al Auliya' ("Memorial of the Saints") by Farid al-Din Attar*. London, 1979.

Asbahānī, Abū Tāhir al-Salafī, al-. *Al-Muntaqā min kitāb makārim al-akhlaq wa maʿlīyuhā wa maḥmūd tarā'iqihā li Abī Bakr Muḥammad ibn Jaʿfar ibn Sahl al-Kharā'itī*, Damascus, 1988.

Azami, M.M. *Studies in Early Hadith Literature*. Indianapolis, 1978.

Bayhaqī, Aḥmad b. al-Ḥusayn, al-. *Shuʿab al-Īmān*. 9 vols. Beirut, 1990/1410.

——*K. al-ādāb*. Beirut, 1988.

Brockelmann, C. *Geschichte der arabischen Litteratur*. 2nd ed. Leiden, 1943-1949; *Supplement*, Leiden, 1937-1942.

Bukhārī, Muḥammad b. Ismāʿīl, al-. *Jāmiʿ al-Ṣaḥīḥ*. Cairo, 1309 AH.

Dermenghem, E. *Vies des saints musulmans*. Paris, 1983.

Encyclopaedia of Islam, 1st ed. by M. Houtsma et al. Leiden, 1927. New edition, ed. by J.H. Kramers, H.A.R. Gibb et al. Leiden, 1954-.

Ghazālī, Abū Ḥāmid Muḥammad b. Muḥammad, al-. *Al-Ghazālī The Remembrance of Death and the Afterlife*. Translated and annotated by T.J. Winter. Cambridge: The Islamic Texts Society, 1989.

——*Al-Ghazālī On Disciplining the Soul & On Breaking the Two Desires*. Translated and annotated by T.J. Winter. Cambridge: The Islamic Texts Society, 1995.

Ḥākim al-Tirmidhī, al-. *Nawādir al-uṣūl fī maʿrifat aḥādīth al-Rasūl*. Ed. ʿAbd al-Raḥmān ʿUmayr. Beirut, 1412/1992.

——Tafsīr al-Qur'ān. In *Mawsūʿat: al-Ḥadīth al-Sharīf* (database of *ḥadīth* on CD ROM). Vol. 1.1. Saudi Arabia: Sakhr Company, 1991-1997.

Ibn ʿAbd al-Barr, Yūsuf. *Al-Inbāh ʿalā qabā'il al-ruwā*. Ed. I. al-Ibyārī. Beirut, 1405/1985.

——*Al-Istīʿāb fī maʿrifat al-Aṣḥāb*. With *al-Iṣāba* of Ibn Ḥajar. Cairo, 1358-9 AH.

Ibn Abi'l-Dunyā, ʿAbd Allāh b. Muḥammad. *K. al-Ṣamt wa ḥifẓ al-lisān*. Ed. and introd. M. A. ʿĀshūr. Cairo, 1406/1986.

Ibn Ḥajar al-ʿAsqalānī, *al-Iṣāba fī tamyīz al-Ṣaḥāba*. Cairo, 1358-9 AH.

——*al-Iṣāba fī tamyīz al-Ṣaḥāba*. Beirut, n.d.

——*Tahdhīb al-Tahdhīb*. Hyderabad, 1326 AH.

Ibn Ḥanbal, Aḥmad b. Muḥammad. *al-Musnad*. Cairo, 1313 AH.

——*K. al-Zuhd*. Beirut, 1994.

Ibn Ḥibbān, Muḥammad, al-Bustī. *Mashāhīr ʿulamā' al-amṣār*. Ed. M. Fleischhammer. Cairo, 1959.

Ibn al-Jawzī. *Manāqib Maʿrūf al-Karkhī wa-akhbāruhu*. Ed. A. al-Jabbūrī. Beirut, 1406/1985.

Ibn al-Jazārī, Shams al-Dīn Muḥammad. *Ghāyat al-nihāya fī ṭabaqāt al-Qurrā'*. Ed. G. Bergsträsser and O. Pretzl. Cairo, 1352/1933.

Ibn Māja al-Qazwīnī, *al-Sunan*. Delhi, 1333 AH.

Ibn al-Nadīm, Muḥammad. *al-Fihrist*. Ed. G. Flügel. Leipzig, 1871-2.

Ibn Qayyim al-Jawziyya. *Al-Wābil al-Ṣayyib wa Rāfiʿ al-Kalimi'l-Tayyib*. Ed. Shaykh Ismāʿīl Muḥammad al-Anṣārī. Riyāḍ, n.d.

——*Zād al-Maʿād fī Hadyī Khayri'l-ʿIbād*. Ed. Shuʿayb and ʿAbd al-Qādir al-Arna'ūṭ. Kuwait, 1412/1992.

Iṣfahānī, Abū Nuʿaym, al-. *Ḥilyat al-awliyā' wa ṭabaqāt al-aṣfiyā'*. Beirut, 1986.

Kharā'iṭī, Muḥammad b. Jaʿfar, al-. *Makārim al-akhlāq wa maʿālīhā*. Ed. ʿAbd Allāh ibn Ḥajjāj. Cairo, 1980.

Khaṭīb al-Baghdādī, al-. *Tārīkh Baghdād*. Cairo, 1349.

Makkī, Abū Ṭālib, al-. *Qūt al-Qulūb*. Beirut, 1997.

Massignon, L. *Essai sur les origines du lexique technique de la mystique musulmane*. 2nd e. Paris, 1954.

Mawsūʿat: al-Ḥadīth al-Sharīf (database of *ḥadīth* on CD ROM). Vol. 1.1. Saudi Arabia: Sakhr Company, 1991-1997.

Murābiṭ, J. al-. *al-Sarī al-Saqaṭī*. Beirut, 1398 AH.

Muslim, b. Ḥajjāj. *Faḍā'il al-Ṣaḥaba*. In *Mawsūʿat: al-Ḥadīth al-Sharīf* (database of *ḥadīth* on CD-ROM). Vol. 1.1. Saudi Arabia: Sakhr Company, 1991-1997.

——*Ṣaḥīḥ*. In *Mawsūʿat: al-Ḥadīth al-Sharīf* (database of *ḥadīth* on CD-ROM). Vol. 1.1. Saudi Arabia: Sakhr Company, 1991-1997.

Nasā'ī, Aḥmad b. Shuʿayb, al-. *al-Ḍuʿafā' wa'l-matrūkīn*. Ed. B. al-Ḍannāwī and K. al-Ḥūt. Beirut, 1405/1985.

——*K. ʿAmali'l-Yawmī wa'l-Laylah*. Beirut, 1406/1986.

Nawawī, Muḥy'l-Dīn Yaḥya, al-. *Tahdhīb al-asmā' wa'l-lughāt*. Ed. F. Wüstenfeld. Göttingen, 1842-7.

——*al-Adhkār*. Cairo, n.d.

Nicholson, R.A., *The Kashf al-maḥjūb the oldest Persian treatise on Sufiism*. Leiden and London, 1911. [Tr. With introd. of the *Kashf al-Maḥjūb* of al-Jullābī al-Hujwīrī.]

Pickthall, Marmaduke. *The Meaning of the Glorious Koran*. London: Allen & Unwin, 1976.

Quḍāʿī, Muḥammad b. Salāma, al-. *Musnad al-Shihāb*. Beirut, 1405/1985.

Al-Qur'ān al-Karīm. CD ROM with commentaries by Jalālayn, Ibn Kathīr and al-Qurṭubī. Vol. 6.31. Saudi Arabia: Sakhr Company, 1996.

Qushayrī, Abu'l al-Qāsim, al-. *Al-Risāla fī ʿilm al-taṣawwuf*. 8th ed. Beirut, n.d.

Sezgin, F. *Geschichte des arabischen Schrifttums*. Leiden 1967-.

Shorter Encyclopaedia of Islam, The. Ed. H.A.R. Gibb and J.H. Kramers. Leiden, 1974.

Sijistānī, Abū Dāūd, al-. *al-Sunan*. Cairo, 1369-70/1950-51.

Ṣafadī, Ṣalāḥ al-Dīn Khalīl b. Aybak al-. *al-Wāfī bi'l-wafayāt*. Ed. H. Ritter et al.. Wiesbaden, 1962-.

Sulamī, Abū ʿAbd al-Raḥmān, al-. *Jawāmiʿ ādāb al-Ṣūfīya*, printed with his *ʿUyūb al-nafs wa-mudāwātuhā*. Ed. & introduced by E. Kohlberg. Jerusalem, 1976.

——*Ṭabaqāt al-Ṣūfīya*. Ed. J. Pedersen. Leiden, 1960.

——*Ṭabaqāt al-Ṣūfīya*. 3rd ed. Cairo, 1997.

ʿUqaylī, Muḥammad b. ʿAmr, al-. *K. al-Ḍuʿafāʾ al-Kabīr*. Ed. A. Qalʿajī. Beirut, 1404/1984.

Ziriklī, Khayr al-Dīn, al-. *Al-Aʿlām*. 10th ed. 8 vols. Beirut, 1995.

GENERAL INDEX

ʿAbd Allāh ibn al-Mubārak, 14, 31
ʿAbd al-Raḥmān ibn Abī Layla, 43
ablution, 4, 15, 25, 36, 52
Abraham, 29,39,38
Abū ʿAlī al-Rūdhbārī, 51
Abū Ayyūb al-Anṣārī, 21
Abū Bakr , 9, 21
Abū Dharr, 20
Abu'l-Haytham ibn al-Tayyihān, 21
Abū Qatāda, 43
Abū Rāfiʿ, 29
Abū Sulaymān al-Dārānī, 39
Abū Turāb al-Nakhshabī, 32
Abū Wā'il, 25
accepting an invitation, xv, 29, 31-35
accompanying guests to the door, 43
affectation in hospitality, 14, 23, 24, 32
Aḥmad ibn Ḥanbal, 37
Aḥmad al-Jalla, 50
ʿĀ'isha, xi, xiii, 39
ʿAlī ibn Abī Ṭālib, 20, 24, 48
al-Aʿmash, 25
Anas ibn Mālik, 4, 7, 15, 24, 30
angels, pray for those at table, 19
ʿAwn ibn ʿAbd Allāh al-Masʿūdī, 21
al-Awzāʿī, xiii, 43

Baghdad, 25
beef, 48
Bishr ibn al-Ḥārith al-Ḥāfī, 50
bisqārjāt, 48
blood vessels, 49
body, things which weaken and strengthen the——, 51
bread, xi, xii, 5, 6, 7, 8, 24, 26, 32, 39, 40, 44, 50
būrāniyya, 39
Burayra, 22

choosing between foods, 25, 38
condiment (*udm* or *idām*), xi, 6, 39, 50
contentment, 39
conversation while eating——, 34, 43
courses, serving all, 40
crumbs, eating——, 10

dates, 8, 13, 14, 24, 48, 49, 50
departing guests, 43
Dhu'l-Nūn al-Miṣrī , 50
drinking, manners relating to——, 9, 10
entering houses, 21-23
expiation, 30

fast, breaking a supererogatory ——, xv, xvi, 33, 34
fast, what to saying upon breaking the——, 11

fish, 40, 48
fruit, eating, 8, 38, 48
al-Fuḍayl ibn ʿIyāḍ, 23

God-fearing, feeding the——, 31

al-Ḥajjāj, 48
Hārūn al-Rashīd, 15
al-Ḥasan al-Baṣrī, 19, 22, 23
al-Ḥasan ibn ʿAlī, 14, 31
haṣramiyya, 39
Ḥātim al-Aṣamm, 38
hospitality, XII, XIII, 2, 20, 29, 30, 34, 36, 40
humility, 4, 16, 44, 47, 48

Ibn ʿAbbās, XIII, XV, 33
Ibn Masʿūd, 15, 42
Ibn ʿUmar, 7, 20, 47
Ibrāhīm ibn Adham, 42
Ibrāhīm ibn Shaybān, 6
ice, drinking water with——, 39
innovations, 5
intention, in giving an invitation, 30
invitation, accepting an——, see accepting

Jābir ibn ʿAbd Allāh, 24, 26
Jaʿfar ibn Abī Ṭālib, 49
Jaʿfar ibn Muḥammad, 'al-Ṣādiq', 14, 19
Jonah (Yūnus), the Prophet, 24
al-Junayd, Abū'l Qāsim, 44

al-Kattānī, Muḥammad ibn ʿAlī, 26
khiwān, 4
Khurāsān, 19
knife, cutting bread or meat with a——, 8
koḥl, offering——to guests, 34
Kurāʿ al-Ghamīm, 33

licking the dish, 10

Mālik ibn Anas, 16, 36
al-Ma'mūn, 39
manna, 39
maraqa, 31
market, eating in the——, 47
Maʿrūf al-Karkhī, 32
Al-Mawṣilī, 50
miḥrāb, 27
milk, what to saying upon drinking——, 11
Muʿāwiya, 15
Muḥammad ibn Wāsiʿ, 22
music, VII, 34

al-Nakhī, Ibrāhīm, 47
Negus, 43
noble character , 20

olives, 40

Paradise, rooms in——, 20
——the food of——, 44
place, being satisfied with, one's——in a gathering, 36
pomegranate, 40
portion of food allotted to family, 42
potash (*ūshnān*), 4, 5, 12
prayer, eating at time of——, 7
presenting what is at hand to eat , 23-25

qibla , 36, 51
quantity of food, 41